T0387016

WRITTEN BY
JUDY NEWMAN COBURN

PHOTOGRAPHY BY
PAUL STRABBING

NICOLE BUJEWSKI
KRISTIN MITCHELL

KEITH BURROWS
LESLIE DAMASO

LITTLE CREEK PRESS
MINERAL POINT, WISCONSIN

Nordic Creamery

Little Creek Press
5341 Sunny Ridge Road
Mineral Point, WI 53565

ORDERING INFORMATION
Quantity sales. Special discounts are available on quantity purchases by corporations, associations, and others. For details, contact info@littlecreekpress.com

Orders by US trade bookstores and wholesalers.
Please contact Little Creek Press or Ingram for details.

Printed in the United States of America

Cataloging-in-Publication Data
Names: Bujewski, Nicole; Burrows, Keith; Damaso, Leslie; Mitchell, Kristin
Title: The Wisconsin Whey: Cheesemaking in the Driftless
Description: Mineral Point, WI | Little Creek Press, 2025
Identifiers: LCCN: 2025931355 | ISBN: 978-1-955656-90-0
Subjects: BUSINESS & ECONOMICS / Industries / Agribusiness
TRAVEL / United States / Midwest
BUSINESS & ECONOMICS / Industries / Food Industry

Book design by Little Creek Press

The
WISCONSIN WHEY

CHEESEMAKING IN THE DRIFTLESS

Thank you to these special supporters:

Steven Bujewski

Christopher Hanger

Andrew and Tiki Randazzo

Ross and Gloria Randazzo

Schroeder Käse

The
WISCONSIN WHEY
CHEESEMAKING IN THE DRIFTLESS

❝Expansive and enthusiastic, *The Wisconsin Whey* profiles the artisan cheesemakers who, as Uplands' Andy Hatch puts it, 'make something delicious and bring people joy.' From fresh cheese curds to 20-year-aged cheddar, each cheese has a story. Learning how they came to be makes them taste that much better. What a fun read!"

—Lindsay Christians, author of *Madison Chefs* and
  The Osteria Papavero Cookbook

❝Where's the epicenter for excellence in Wisconsin cheesemaking? Tough question! *The Wisconsin Whey* makes quietly compelling arguments for the rural southwest, where lovely landscapes and tiny towns rule."

—Mary Bergin, author of *Small-Town Wisconsin* and
  Wisconsin Supper Club Cookbook

❝Seriously, what a lactic legacy! Make yourself a cheese board, and tuck into this book.”

—Tenaya Darlington, author of *Madame Fromage's Adventures in Cheese* and cheese educator

❝What a wonderful depiction of the innovation and creativity of 12 of Wisconsin's most notable cheesemakers. *The Wisconsin Whey* digs well beyond the surface to deliver a tome fraught with insights into the history and evolution of the state's inimitable cheese culture.

Cheese lovers will treasure this inside look into the unique combination of terroir, tenacity, passion, and collegiality that coalesce to form the magic behind some of the state's most distinctive cheeses.”

—Lori Fredrich, OnMilwaukee.com dining concierge and author of *Wisconsin Field to Fork*

❝*The Wisconsin Whey* aims a proud, joyful lens on a prime cheesemaking region and gives its most accomplished producers their well-deserved due. We know that the pleasure of eating, as Wendell Berry famously noted, has much to do with 'one's accurate consciousness of the lives and the world from which food comes.' And sure enough, the passion, intelligence, and accomplishment revealed in this book just made my dairyland cheeseboard taste even better than ever.”

—Terese Allen, author of *The Flavor of Wisconsin* and *The Dane County Farmers' Market Cookbook*

Hidden Springs Creamery

TABLE OF CONTENTS

Uplands Cheese

FOREWORD BY JERRY APPS

I have fond memories of growing up on a small dairy farm in central Wisconsin in the late 1930s and 1940s, where we milked cows by hand with the light of kerosene barn lanterns. I fondly remember the time when I traveled with my dad to the Wild Rose Cheese Factory on a cold winter day. The men were working with huge vats of milk.

"What are they doing?" I asked my dad.

"Making cheese," my dad said, smiling. "Turning our milk into cheese."

One of the cheesemakers handed me a piece of irregularly shaped, warm material.

"Here," he said. "Take a bite," which I did. It made a squeaky noise when I bit into it, but it tasted okay. It was like nothing I'd ever tasted before.

"What is it?" I asked.

"It's a cheese curd," the cheesemaker said.

That was my first introduction to cheesemaking. Cheese was regularly offered at our dinner table, but it was yellow, sometimes white, and didn't look at all like the cheese curd I had tasted at the cheese factory.

In this book, readers will learn about the wonderful variety of Wisconsin-made cheeses, many made by the cheesemakers in the Driftless Area (southwestern Wisconsin).

But first let's go back in Wisconsin's history for a bit, as we today applaud Wisconsin as the leading cheese producer in the nation. As a long-time rural historian, when I read history, I want to see the context for what I am reading. I want to know what led up to what is happening now. In this foreword, I describe the major historical events that occurred in Wisconsin, eventually leading to the development of a highly successful cheesemaking industry. Dairy farming and cheesemaking were not a part of Wisconsin's early history. Indeed, in Wisconsin's early years, dairy cows and cheesemaking were mostly nonexistent.

Here is a brief review of early Wisconsin history. The last major glaciers began melting about 10,000 to 12,000 years ago (except for the Driftless region of Wisconsin, which recent glaciers spared). These glaciers left behind the hills and valleys, rivers and lakes, sometimes rich soil and, in other places, soil not so rich in much of Wisconsin. After the glaciers retreated, some two-thirds of the state became forested. At that time, much of southern Wisconsin was prairie with occasional oak trees.

Native Americans began arriving in what is now Wisconsin shortly after the glaciers' retreat. Not until 1634 did the first European, Jean Nicolet, arrive in the state. Other French explorers began what became known as the Fur Trading Era, where the explorers traded various goods with Native Americans for mostly beaver pelts.

The Lead Mining Era emerged between 1804 and 1832 in southwestern Wisconsin. It soon became the predominant economic activity in the state. Most of northern Wisconsin continued to be Native American lands.

Wisconsin became a territory in 1836 and a state in 1848. By the time Wisconsin achieved statehood in 1848, the Lead Mining Era was about over. At the time of statehood, several of the state's politicians and other business leaders began recognizing the value of the forest lands in the north. Following several Native American treaties, the north was opened up to widespread logging operations. Thus, Wisconsin's Logging Era began, which continued into the early 1900s. Similar to the lead mining industry, with the introduction of clear-cutting, the logging industry could not be sustained, and it diminished.

After more treaties with the Native Americans and a government survey completed in 1836, settlers began arriving in southeastern Wisconsin and buying the recently surveyed land. Some early settlers arrived from upstate New York and New England. A large percentage of these new arrivals were farmers, looking for new agricultural lands and leaving behind what they referred to as "worn-out land."

A number of the settlers from New England and Upstate New York, had been dairy farmers. But once arriving in Wisconsin they became wheat farmers. The Midwest was becoming a major wheat-growing region. Illinois and Indiana farmers were major wheat growers, and the new settlers in Wisconsin soon joined them. Some of these early wheat farmers grew up to 50 acres of wheat. They continued growing wheat on the same wheat fields year after year. By 1850, wheat growing expanded across the state and became Wisconsin's major economic enterprise—the Wheat Growing Era.

By the 1870s, wheat growing began declining. Farmers planted wheat on the same field year after year, resulting in a steady decline in soil fertility and declining wheat yields. Disease and insect problems contributed to the yield problem. By 1879, wheat growing was on its way out. But what next? Farmers had to make a living. Some took up raising sheep—wool prices soared during the Civil War (1861–1865). Some farmers grew barley and hops for the fast-growing brewing industry. Some grew tobacco. None of these alternative crops proved as profitable as wheat had been.

Those settlers from New York, who had been dairy farmers there, began once more to milk cows. But most of the once well-to-do wheat farmers resisted becoming dairy farmers. These former wheat farmers believed that caring for cows was women's work. Many of the former wheat farmers did own a cow or two. But the women cared for them, fed them, milked them, and made butter and cheese in the farm kitchen. Also, becoming a dairy farmer meant milking cows every day of the year without exception. Wheat farmers enjoyed having little farm work to do during Wisconsin's long winters. It took about 20 years before milking cows and making cheese became a primary agricultural activity in Wisconsin.

Former New Yorkers, such as William Dempster Hoard and several others, helped Wisconsin fledgling dairy farmers learn the ins and outs of dairy farming. One important thing these former New Yorkers shared was the need to build a barn to house the cattle during Wisconsin's long, cold winters. The building had to be more than a drafty shed, which was the kind of housing wheat farmers often provided for their cow or two. Soon we began seeing the construction of beautiful big barns. Many may be seen in parts of the state today. Dairy cows needed something to eat, and a lot of it. The early dairy farmers learned about growing hay crops such as alfalfa and clover, which could be made into hay and stored in the upper reaches of the big barns. What were once wheat fields were now turned into cow pastures and hay fields—fertilized by cow manure.

Cheese and buttermaking remained in the farm kitchen, the work done by women, as these activities were not considered proper work for men. It took a while, but when men decided it was appropriate for them to make cheese, they wanted to do it away from the farm kitchen. Thus, the early cheese factory was born, many located at a crossroads and sometimes only two miles apart. This allowed farmers with their teams and wagons a short trip to a cheese factory with their milk. The National Historic Cheesemaking Center offered this: "By 1899, Wisconsin contained 1,500 cheese factories located at rural crossroads where farmers would deliver their daily milk. Cheese production was 77,848,600 pounds. The top-producing cheese state at the turn of the twentieth century was New York. Wisconsin had already passed Ohio (1880) and eventually surpassed New York by 1910, becoming number one in cheese production in the USA."[1]

According to the Wisconsin Historical Society, "Charles Rockwell was among the state's earliest cheesemakers, beginning production at Koshkonong near Fort Atkinson in 1837. Using milk from neighbors' cows, Anne Pickett established a cheese factory in Lake Mills in 1841."[2]

With the creative development of many new cheese varieties and a strong marketing effort, per capita cheese consumption continues to increase, reaching record numbers each year. In 2023, U.S. citizens consumed, on average, 42.3 pounds of cheese per capita, another new record.[3]

Wisconsin's historic cheese varieties include cheddar, Swiss, Limburger, Parmesan, Monterey Jack, and mozzarella. Two historic cheeses were created in Wisconsin. Colby, a cheddar-like cheese, but softer and open-textured, was developed in the Colby community in the north central part of the state. Brick cheese, the second Wisconsin original, is a semisoft open-textured cheese created by cheesemaker John Jossi in Dodge County.

For many years, cheddar was the most popular cheese produced in Wisconsin. In the 1950s, with the increasing popularity of pizza, mozzarella began to climb in popularity, and today mozzarella cheese has pushed cheddar into second place in

---

1   https://nationalhistoriccheesemakingcenter.org/history-of-cheese/.

2   Historical Essay, Cheesemaking in Wisconsin, Wisconsin Historical Society, https://www.wisconsinhistory.org/Records/Article/CS1896.

3   Teodora Lyubomirova, "Five takeaways from the latest USDA dairy consumption data," *Dairy Reporter*, December 2, 2024, https://www.dairyreporter.com/Article/2024/12/02/us-2023-dairy-consumption-data-more-cheese-less-ice-cream/.

terms of the amount produced by Wisconsin cheesemakers. In 2025, Wisconsin produced 600 different varieties of cheese.

I'll end this foreword with a bit of a cheesy story. Several years ago, a California television reporter interviewed me about one of my agricultural history books. She asked, "Aren't you a bit embarrassed when people call you a Cheesehead?"

"Not a bit," I answered. "I'm rather proud to be called a Cheesehead."

She was stopped cold for several moments, unable to think of a follow-up question.

Earlier, I'd looked up the history of the foam Cheesehead that Wisconsin people sometimes wear at sports events. The following is from my book *Cheese: The Making of a Wisconsin Tradition:*

> The idea of a Cheesehead as something to wear on your head belongs to Ralph Bruno. He founded the Foamation Company in Milwaukee in 1987 when he was about 26 years old. He'd been helping his mother reupholster her couch, working with foam rubber. With a knife he cut a piece of foam into a triangular shape, painted it yellow, cut some holes in it, and put it on his head. He wore the oddity to a Brewer game and saw his buddies scatter when the opposing team's fans called him a Cheesehead. But the strange looking headpiece was capturing attention. People made fun of it, but they were also intrigued. These reactions were enough to cause Bruno to think about a possible, albeit rather far out idea for making and marketing the triangular piece of yellow foam…. Having a background in pattern and mold making, he had the necessary technical skills (to make them)…. When the Green Bay Packers played in Super Bowl XXXI (1997) in New Orleans, Bruno, a forever Packers fan, decided to haul a semi-load of foam Cheeseheads to New Orleans…. He attended a

big Packers fan party and sold $10 Cheeseheads one after the other. It was the turning point for Cheesehead sales. The Cheesehead continued to grow in popularity.

Hats off to the cheesemakers of Wisconsin's Driftless region. Their contributions to Wisconsin's cheesemaking industry are enormous.

 Jerry Apps, a rural historian, has written several books and narrated PBS documentaries on rural Midwestern history. For this foreword, Apps has drawn on *Cheese, The Making of a Wisconsin Tradition*, second edition (2020); *Wisconsin Agriculture: A History* (2015); *Barns of Wisconsin* (2010); and *When the White Pine Was King: A History of Lumberjacks, Log Drives, and Sawdust Cities in Wisconsin* (2020).

About 90 percent of the milk produced in Wisconsin is made into cheese.

The Driftless Area

INTRODUCTION

When you think of Wisconsin, what's the first thing that comes to mind?

It could be the beauty of nature, the abundance of indoor water parks, or maybe the Green Bay Packers or the University of Wisconsin Badgers.

But most likely, it's cheese.

Wisconsin is the number one cheese-producing state in the nation. The state is home to nearly 1,200 cheesemakers who produce more than 600 varieties of cheese—nearly twice as many as any other state, according to the Wisconsin Department of Agriculture, Trade and Consumer Protection.[1]

A quarter of all the cheese produced in the entire U.S. is made in Wisconsin. That amounted to more than 3.5 billion pounds in 2023.[2]

It's no wonder that Wisconsin is known as America's Dairyland … and its unofficial apparel accessory is the bright yellow foam cheesehead hat.

Mineral Point residents Nicole Bujewski, owner of The Book Kitchen culinary school; Keith Burrows and Leslie Damaso, owners of Republic of Letters independent bookstore; and

---

1   https://datcp.wi.gov/Pages/Publications/WIAgStatistics.aspx.

2   https://www.nass.usda.gov/Statistics_by_State/Wisconsin/Publications/Dairy/2024/WI-SpecialtyCheese-05-24.pdf.

Kristin Mitchell, Little Creek Press book publisher, wanted to highlight and celebrate some of the cheesemakers in the state—specifically those in the Driftless Area, which includes Mineral Point. The Driftless is a long swath of western Wisconsin whose hills and valleys, untouched by the glaciers that raked through much of the eastern portions of the state thousands of years ago, retain the natural beauty and the rich soil that drew settlers to the state a few centuries ago.

Many of the finest cheese artisans in the nation choose to live and work in the Driftless, and their cheeses have won hundreds of awards in state, national, and world competitions. The cheesemakers will tell you that milk produced in the Driftless is a big reason why their cheeses are so flavorful and highly acclaimed.

With help from Joe Burns, co-owner of Brunkow Cheese in Fayette, 12 cheesemakers were chosen to feature in this book about cheesemakers in the Driftless. They are not the only expert cheesemakers in the region, but they represent a range of the current industry trends. Five of them had their cheeses featured on *Top Chef: Wisconsin,* the Bravo TV competition that filmed its 21st season in Wisconsin and aired in spring 2024.

Paul Strabbing, an award-winning food photographer based in Chicago, has captured the essence of these artisans and their cheese creations through his visuals, and Judy Newman Coburn, a former business reporter for the *Wisconsin State Journal*, is telling their stories.

We will introduce you to Wisconsin Master Cheesemaker Sid Cook, whose 50-plus varieties of Carr Valley Cheese have won more national and international awards than any other cheese company in North America; Master Cheesemaker Andy Hatch, whose Pleasant Ridge Reserve—one of only two cheeses produced by Uplands Cheese—has brought home more awards than any other individual cheese in the U.S.; and Master Cheesemaker Tony Hook of Hook's Cheese, who broke records with his 20-year-aged cheddar.

They are Wisconsin Master Cheesemakers, a trademarked title because, in addition to their years of experience, they have gone through rigorous coursework and exams to earn that distinction. Wisconsin is the only state to require its cheesemakers to be licensed. Becoming a master is a step well beyond.

As we traveled through western Wisconsin, from Shullsburg, near the Illinois border, to Westby, about 100 miles to the north, we met some cheesemakers who are carrying on three or four generations of a legacy in the business and others who stumbled into it 10 years ago or less. They include women who are breaking into the largely male-dominated field, those who use milk only from cows, and those who focus on sheep's or goat's milk. One has even experimented with water buffalo's milk. The backgrounds of these cheesemakers are diverse: one was a lawyer and economist, another worked on political campaigns, a third was a wine marketer, and one began making goat's milk cheese due to his infant son's lactose intolerance.

What we found is a somewhat eclectic bunch of artisans with varying interests and backgrounds who work long hours and take great pride in their dedication to quality and in their craftsmanship. We also found an extraordinary sense of cooperation, collaboration, mentorship, camaraderie, and friendship among these people, which would likely be hard to replicate in any other industry or any other place.

We hope you will enjoy getting to know them.

Cedar Grove Cheese

WISCONSIN'S CHEESE LEGACY

Cheese has played a starring role in Wisconsin's story, from the early days through the present, and will continue to do so well into the future.

The Badger State may no longer have a tavern (or two), a church, and a cheese factory in every town, but the cheesemaking that is going on today is inventive and intentional, and is drawing attention to Wisconsin because of its craftsmanship as well as quantity.

Consider this: Feld restaurant in Chicago held a cheese dinner in which all but three of the more than 20 courses on the tasting menu included Uplands Cheese's Pleasant Ridge Reserve or Rush Creek Reserve. The Deliciouser in Madison staged a similar event, with Uplands cheeses listed in seven of its courses.

Chicago restaurants have been aware of the high quality of Wisconsin cheeses for a long time, says Joe Burns, co-owner of Brunkow Cheese in Fayette. "If you order a cheese plate [in a Chicago restaurant], you'll more often than not see that Wisconsin artisanal cheese is on the board," he says.

The state's cheese reputation, in fact, carries around the globe. John Umhoefer, executive director of the Wisconsin Cheese Makers Association, says that in his travels to Europe or the Pacific Rim, people talk about Wisconsin, not the U.S., as the home of cheesemaking. "Wisconsin is really understood to be on par with cheeses made around the world," he says.

Ken Monteleone, owner of Fromagination in Madison, says he opened his specialty cheese shop in 2007 precisely because he wanted to honor the area's cheesemaking legacy and innovations. "I fell in love with the passion of our tradition here in Wisconsin. I wanted to help advocate for this rich tradition of cheesemaking. Little did I know I'd meet some wonderful people along the way," Monteleone says.

DRIFTLESS IMPACT

With its striking and significant topography and geology, the Driftless Area plays a large part in the state's cheese industry, especially now, as more cheesemakers produce artisan products with unique appearances, flavors, and characteristics.

The Driftless refers to a stretch of southwestern and western Wisconsin untouched by the last glaciers thousands of years ago. The glaciers flattened terrain and moved around soil, rocks, and minerals, known as drift. The Driftless retained its hills and valleys, and the rich soil that covers them.

"It really affects our grasses, flowers, and everything that grows in our area," says Tony Hook, owner of Hook's Cheese in Mineral Point. "I think the Driftless region is about the best area to make cheese in this country. As the glaciers came through, they dragged things through other areas of the country with them, where our land probably hasn't changed in a million years."

And it's not just the topography. There's a special culture to the Driftless, says Andy Hatch, co-owner of Uplands Cheese near Dodgeville.

"The soil and water quality and the climate and rainfall are the foundation of Driftless cheese, but so are the people and the types of businesses you find here. The tight hills mean that farms can't get very big, and so neither have most of the cheesemakers. We've had to focus on being unique, and luckily, we have interesting terroir to make that possible," Hatch says.

WE'RE NO. 1

Here are some impressive statistics that demonstrate why Wisconsin is the cheese capital of the U.S.:

About 90 percent of the milk produced in Wisconsin is made into cheese.

Wisconsin produced more cheese than any other state in 2023—a lot more. Wisconsin cheesemakers produced 3.5 billion pounds of cheese, which amounted to 25 percent of all the cheese made nationwide that year.[1] The No. 2 cheese-producing state was California, which made 2.5 billion pounds, according to the USDA's Dairy Products Annual Report.[2] All of the other states lagged far behind.

More than one-fourth (27 percent) of the cheese made in Wisconsin in 2023 was specialty cheese, totaling 942 million pounds—also the highest of any state.[3] Specialty cheese is defined as a high-quality, premium-priced cheese that may have exotic origins, special processing or design, limited supply, unusual use, and extraordinary packaging.

Wisconsin makes about 50 percent of all the specialty cheeses in the U.S., says Dean Sommer, cheese technologist at

---

1   https://datcp.wi.gov/Pages/Publications/WIAgStatistics.aspx.

2   USDA/NASS, Dairy Products Annual Summary, 4/26/2024, https://usda.library.cornell.edu/concern/publications/jm214p131.

3   https://www.nass.usda.gov/Statistics_by_State/Wisconsin/Publications/Dairy/2024/WI-SpecialtyCheese-05–24.pdf.

UW–Madison's Center for Dairy Research (CDR). "That's a credit to our cheesemakers, their skills, and the innovation they have." he says.

The dairy industry contributes $52.8 billion to Wisconsin's economy annually, which is comparable to the annual revenue of major companies such as Nike and American Airlines.[4] In fact, dairy produces more revenue for Wisconsin than citrus for Florida and potatoes for Idaho combined, according to the CDR.[5]

If Wisconsin were a country, it would be the fourth-largest cheesemaking country in the world, behind only the U.S., Germany, and France.[6]

LICENSE REQUIRED

One reason that Wisconsin cheesemakers are so highly regarded is: They know what they're doing. Wisconsin is the only state in the nation that requires its cheesemakers to be licensed, which means they have to take specific courses about cheese production, sanitation, science, and safety; complete at least 240 hours of on-the-job training; and then pass a written exam.

"I think it does show in their cheeses," Umhoefer says. "I think it also makes cheesemaking more of a profession or a craft. A cheesemaker in Wisconsin thinks of himself or herself as a craftsperson rather than someone who has a job. It's an identity."

---

4 Dr. Steven Deller, et al., "The Contribution of Dairy to the Wisconsin Economy," November 2022, ContributionOfDairyToWisconsinEconomy_2024.pdf.

5 National Potato Council, "Measuring the Economic Significance of the U.S. Potato Industry, https://www.nationalpotatocouncil.org/wp-content/uploads/2023/02/NPCSpudNationReport.pdf; USDA/NASS, Potatoes 2021 Summary, https://usda.library.cornell.edu/concern/publications/fx719m44h; Julio Cruz, et al., "2020–2021 Economic Contributions of the Florida Citrus Industry," https://fred.ifas.ufl.edu/media/fredifasufledu/economic-impact-analysis/reports/FRE_Economic_Contributions_Florida_Citrus_Industry_Report_2020_21_WEB-(2).pdf.

6 USDA/NASS, Dairy Products Annual Summary, 4/26/2024, https://usda.library.cornell.edu/concern/publications/jm214p131; Eurostat, Milk collection (all milks) and dairy products obtained – annual data, DOI: 10.2908/apro_mk_pobta.

On top of licensing, experienced cheesemakers can become Wisconsin Master Cheesemakers—a title considered so special that it's trademarked. Wisconsin and Switzerland are the only places in the world that offer this advanced ranking.

The program is conducted in Wisconsin through the Center for Dairy Research, UW–Extension, and Dairy Farmers of Wisconsin. To qualify, cheesemakers must have been licensed for at least 10 years and must be making a specific cheese for at least five years. They have to take about six advanced courses, host two site visits, and pass a complex test. It takes nearly three years to make it through the Wisconsin Master Cheesemaker program.

The written exam alone consists of essay questions that take 40 to 60 hours to complete. "It's an intense program," Sommer says.

Bob Wills, owner of Cedar Grove Cheese, agrees. "Actually, the two-week take-home final was harder than any other exam I have taken," says Wills, who also has a law degree and a PhD.

There are about 1,200 licensed cheesemakers in Wisconsin,[7] and only 107 have earned a Master Cheesemaker designation since the program began 30 years ago, according to Dairy Farmers of Wisconsin.[8]

Earning a Master's is an honor and a distinction, Sommer says. "They're the best of the best—there's no question about it."

FIRST CHEESE FACTORIES

Cheesemaking started in Wisconsin even before it became a state in 1848.

There's conflicting information as far as when and where the

---

7   https://datcp.wi.gov/Pages/Publications/WIAgStatistics.aspx.

8   There are about 1,200 licensed cheesemakers in Wisconsin,7 and only 96 have earned a Master Cheesemaker designation since the program began 30 years ago, according to Dairy Farmers of Wisconsin.

first cheesemaker began operating in the state.

The State Historical Society says Charles Rockwell was among the state's earliest cheesemakers and began producing cheese at Koshkonong, near Fort Atkinson, in 1837.[9]

Anne Pickett is also mentioned. She established a cheese factory in Lake Mills in 1841, using milk from neighbors' cows.

Others point to Chester Hazen, a New York transplant who started a cheese factory in 1864 in Ladoga, in Fond du Lac County. A plaque on a boulder marks the site of Hazen's cheese plant and calls him the "Father of Wisconsin's Cheese Industry." That was probably the first "true cheese factory," the State Historical Society says.

By the end of the Civil War, in 1865, Wisconsin already had 30 cheese factories.

According to the Center for Dairy Research, the peak came in 1922, when 2,807 cheese plants were operating in Wisconsin and producing about 275.5 million pounds of cheese a year. By 1992, the number of cheese factories had dropped dramatically to 162, but they were making more than two billion pounds a year.[10]

Today, there are about 120 licensed cheese plants, producing 3.5 billion pounds.

FROM BREAD TO CHEESE

Before the Civil War, though, it wasn't cheese that defined Wisconsin. It was wheat.

---

9   "Historical Essay, Dairy Farming in Wisconsin: How Wisconsin Became the Dairy State," Wisconsin Historical Society, https://www.wisconsinhistory.org/Records/Article/CS1744#:~:-text=Charles%20Rockwell%20was%20one%20of,a%20profitable%20way%20to%20farm.

10 USDA/NASS, Dairy Products Annual Summary, 5/1/1993, https://usda.library.cornell.edu/concern/publications/jm214p131; USDA/AMS, "Revisios in the Production of Creamery Butter, Cheese, and Ice Cream, by States, 1916–1939," https://babel.hathitrust.org/cgi/pt?id=uc1.31175022285855&seq=1.

From the 1840s to the 1860s, the state's top agricultural product was wheat, Sommer says. "Wisconsin, at that time, was the breadbasket of the U.S." That is, until the chinch bugs converged on fields across the state. The small, black insects with white wings decimated much of the wheat crop in the 1860s, says Sommer. In addition, the soil's nutrients became depleted, as farmers had been planting on the same fields, year after year, and wore out the soil for wheat.

W.D. Hoard is credited with saving the state's ag economy. Hoard had come to Wisconsin from New York State, where he saw similar events unfold. "His motto was: 'Substitute the cow for the plow,' and he pushed for dairy farming," Sommer says. The timing turned out well, as immigrants arriving from Europe brought with them dairy farming and cheesemaking skills. Thus, the Dairy State took hold.

PIVOTING TO ARTISAN CHEESES

Progress eventually led the cheese industry down some back roads, though. In the 1920s, transportation was limited, and many people in Wisconsin were still getting around in horse-drawn wagons, Sommer says. "There were cheese factories at every major crossroad in dairy farming areas. Farmers had to haul their own milk to the factory. If it was too far, they couldn't afford to waste that much of the day getting to and from the factory."

That changed with the growing use of cars and trucks, the construction of highways, and rural electrification in the 1930s. The number of cheese factories declined, and the remaining ones were larger.

Then came some economic challenges from the East and West. In the 1960s, Europe encroached on the U.S. cheese market, particularly Switzerland, which sent a lot of its government-subsidized cheese here. "The Monroe area was hit hard; cheesemakers there couldn't compete," Sommer says. Those that survived were able to innovate and change products.

A decade or so later, in the 1970s and '80s, western states such as California, Idaho, and New Mexico built up their dairy industries. That had a big impact on the dozens of Wisconsin dairies that were making large quantities of cheddar cheese in 500-pound barrels and selling it to corporations that would grind it up and process it into other products, like American cheese slices or fast-food fare.

When the western states amped up their cheese manufacturing, they could sell at a lower price because the weather was milder and the farms were bigger, providing an economy of scale. "So, people here in Wisconsin had to switch to something else," Sommer says.

In the 1990s, the industry faced a crossroads. Milk production was falling, and Wisconsin was making mostly commodity-style cheeses, such as mozzarella used on pizza and mild cheddar served shredded in salad bars or sliced for food service sandwiches.

"We had the generations of expertise, but we needed to pivot to the higher-value specialty cheese," Umhoefer says.

"There really was a renaissance of cheese production in the state, with many cheesemakers reconfiguring their production from cheeses like cheddar to feta and Havarti," he says. "Also, cheddar that's made for aging is a Wisconsin specialty. It requires a lot of skill to control the flavor across the years."

Other cheeses began to show up more, too, including blue, fontina, Parmesan, and provolone, "with the understanding that we had the skill, and it's time for Wisconsin to take the high ground," Umhoefer says.

CHEESE FOR THE FUTURE AND FOR FUN

Another advantage Wisconsin cheeses have may be imperceptible to the eye or the taste buds. It is the true camaraderie among cheesemakers. "There's definitely a pride that elevates the art," Umhoefer says. "Being craftsmen [and women], there's a unique collaboration that baffles other industries that we talk to. Cheesemakers really talk to each other and help each other—in times of need and in creativity."

"The network of our cheese community is very impressive," adds Fromagination's Monteleone. "They are willing to work side by side and collaborate to make their cheese better and to mentor people getting into the industry."

Having the Center for Dairy Research is also a big plus. The CDR's experts actually make house calls—as doctors did years ago. "They drive to cheese factories and help people with problems," Umhoefer says.

It's all part of helping to train the next generation to carry on the cheesemaking legacy, says the CDR's Sommer.

As Wisconsin cheesemakers branch out into new concepts and improve on the old, chefs and cheesemongers tout the taste and versatility of the artisan products.

"Try a bunch of cheeses and figure out what you like," says Chef Dan Jacobs, owner of DanDan and EsterEv restaurants in Milwaukee and *Top Chef: Wisconsin* runner-up.

Photo credit: Clay Williams

Jacobs says he and his wife, Kate, often put together cheese plates at home with a variety of hard and soft cow's, goat's, and sheep's milk cheeses. "It's our favorite thing to do on Sundays: have a cheese plate and chill.

"I think the most fun thing is just eating a bunch of cheese. I can't see a better day," Jacobs says.

BLEU MONT DAIRY
WILLI LEHNER

Willi Lehner's cheesemaking superpower lies beneath the ground and tucked into a hillside.

Lehner's Bleu Mont Dairy has a cheese cave to be envied—an immaculate, domed structure where his cheeses can serenely age in a stable environment. It is sort of a Taj Mahal of cheese aging facilities.

"That's where the magic happens," Lehner says.

A small Buddha statue perched on one of the staircase-like boulders piled along the outside of the cave and a quartz crystal buried beneath it probably don't hurt, either.

Lehner calls himself a cheesemaker/*affineur*. An *affineur* is the French term for a person who handles and ages cheese, a process called *affinage*. Lehner is low-key in demeanor with a hippie-type vibe, but he is serious about his cheese. And it pays off. Bleu Mont's cheeses draw accolades from near and far.

A *New York Times* article once called Lehner "the off-the-grid rock star of the Wisconsin artisanal cheese movement,"[1] and *Bon Appétit* magazine listed Bleu Mont bandaged cheddar as one of the "25 most important cheeses of America" in a 2018 article.[2]

Bleu Mont's bandaged cheddar helped Tory Miller, executive chef and co-owner of the famed L'Etoile restaurant in Madison,

---

1   Christine Muhlke, "Push Comes to Chèvre," *New York Times*, March 30, 2008, https://www.nytimes.com/2008/03/30/style/tmagazine/30wisconsin.html.

2   Carey Polis, "25 Most Important Cheeses of America, According to Cheese Experts," *Bon Appétit*, April 25, 2018, https://www.bonappetit.com/gallery/most-important-chees-es-in-america?srsltid=AfmBOoodIn_5IUa5ig_joqXf7YVzAuJwdTpDlzZoDLQMX9_NBIHFaM5R.

beat Bobby Flay in the Food Network show *Iron Chef Showdown*. Miller says he's had a relationship with Willi and "his amazing cheeses" for 25 years.

"I've always looked at Wisconsin cheese as my ace in the hole, and the bandaged cheddar has such a distinct flavor, reminiscent of Parmigiano Reggiano. The aging and concentration of flavors, and the unique flavor that Willi's cave imparts, made me think of that cheese when we were creating the gnocchi dish for Battle of Bison," says Miller. "We knew that with it, we had a chance to beat Bobby Flay!"

Lehner modestly shrugs off the praise. "It's like a falling star—it shines brightly for a short time, and then it's gone."

In his early years, Lehner spent some time as a cheesemaker in Switzerland and a traveler exploring Europe and Asia before he settled down back in Wisconsin. His home, off a rural road in southwest Dane County, reflects his interest in nature and his strong belief in sustainability.

Oh, and Willi has another superpower: he yodels.

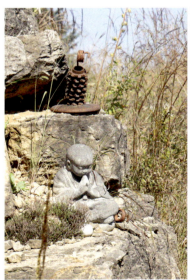

A FAMILY ENDEAVOR

Lehner grew up around cheesemaking. His parents immigrated to the U.S. from Switzerland, and his father, Billi, learned cheesemaking there during a four-year apprenticeship. Billi made the classic Emmental Swiss and Gruyère. When Billi came to North America, he bounced around Canada at first, working in lumber camps in British Columbia and on a farm in Quebec. Then he heard that Wisconsin was looking for cheesemakers, and he jumped at the opportunity.

Billi Lehner made cheese at several factories across southwestern Wisconsin; his longest stint was at Ryser Brothers, where he served as manager and head cheesemaker. Ryser operated in the building, built in 1916, that used to house the Mount Horeb Creamery and Cheese Company and now is home to the Grumpy Troll brewpub. That's where Willi got his start in the cheese business, hanging out in the plant during his childhood and later working for his dad at Ryser and at another cheese factory that Billi bought with other family members.

"I definitely fell into it by default. As little kids in a cheese factory with our dad, my brothers and I did a lot of cleaning and organizing, washing floors, making boxes for packaging. I got my hands in the vat when I was about 14 or 15, aiding in production" under the supervision of a licensed cheesemaker. About a week after the cheeses were made, some were dipped into hot wax as a protective coating. "Those were the best cheddars," Willi says. "That was one of the reasons I decided, years later, to go into bandaged cheddar. Hardly anyone was doing it at the time, around 2004. It was too labor-intensive; only one or two cheesemakers in the country were making it."

Working at his father's factory—now run by Willi's nieces and nephews as Forgotten Valley Cheese—Willi made brick and Muenster cheeses and started experimenting with cheddar cultures. "But we didn't have the right equipment to make cheddar. It worked well enough that it tasted like cheddar, but legally, it wasn't. State rules specify how cheddar must be produced and that it has to be identified not just as 'cheddar' but as 'cheddar cheese.'"

Already armed with a cheesemaker's license, Willi branched out and started his own cheese business. "That was around 1986. But this is actually my 45th year making cheese."

Willi is the oldest of six siblings. At one point, there were four licensed cheesemakers in his immediate family. "Now, I'm the last one standing."

PRODUCING SPECIALTY CHEESE

Bleu Mont Dairy is located in the scenic rolling hills of Blue Mounds, where Lehner lives and ages his cheese—he makes only cheddar-based cheeses and Havarti. Lehner is very deliberate about when he makes the cheese: from May to June and September to October. "I feel that's when the pasture is the best.

"What makes the cheese is the quality of the milk—what the cows are eating and how mineralized the soil is. It's very crucial for top-quality cheese," he says.

Lehner gets milk from Henning Cheese, a four-generation cheesemaking operation in Kiel, about 30 miles northeast of Fond du Lac. Henning's milk comes from 20 nearby family farms. "In the past, I used milk from Uplands Cheese—they've got the best milk around. But now, they're using all of their milk for their own cheese."

Lehner does not have his own cheese factory; he does his production at Henning or Cedar Grove Cheese in Plain. "I arrange with the plant manager to make a batch of cheese. They know the quality of the milk I want and the time of year I want to work there. I reserve the time slot up to six months ahead."

CULTURES COUNT

On production day at Henning, Lehner works with Wisconsin Master Cheesemaker Kerry Henning. "My forte is tweaking things to get the desired result. I use very specific rennet [an enzyme that makes milk coagulate] and adjunct cultures for flavor," he says.

"I use a culture that has a small amount of helveticus in it. Helveticus is a lactic acid bacteria that gives cheese a brothy, umami flavor. Another culture I use is protective and allows cheese to age at an elevated temperature [higher than common refrigeration temperatures of 35 to 40 degrees] without creating the undesirable, gas-producing bacteria that can ruin the cheese," Lehner says.

When Lehner's cheddar is formed into wheels, the bandage—an unbleached muslin-cotton cloth—is pressed onto the cheese, protecting it as it ages. "Cheddar is known to crack if the humidity makes large swings, or if the rind dries too fast, and if that happens, undesirable mold will grow into the cheese," Lehner says. After the bound rounds have aged for almost two weeks, Lehner takes them to his cheese cave in Blue Mounds,

Bandaged Cheddar
@ Hennings

Jun 05, 2024

where they sit on cedar and pine planks for at least 14 months. The average temperature in the cave is 55 degrees, and humidity is 85 to 90 percent.

"Within a month, the cheese is completely covered with molds which produce tremendous flavor. We turn the wheels regularly. The enzymes and molds transform, and the flavor gets more and more complex," Lehner says.

He also vacuums—yes, vacuums!—the wheels, using a heavy-duty commercial vacuum with a bristled head. Not that dust or dirt could find its way into the cave, but rather: cheese mites. "They are a natural and inevitable part of affinage with some cheeses, typically those aged longer at elevated temperatures," Lehner says.

Every two to three months, the bandaged cheddar is vacuumed— eight wheels at a time, removed from a shelf, put onto a cart, and stacked into two piles. The shelf is vacuumed and so is each wheel, individually. One rack takes five or six hours to clean, which means each wheel has been vacuumed about five times by the time it is sold.

THE RESULT

The cheddar that emerges from the bandages is white, with a rich, earthy flavor with hints of umami, he says. *Bon Appétit* says Bleu Mont's cheddar "brims with nutty and caramel overtones alongside the traditional earthy ones."[3]

Big Sky Grana starts out with the same process, but it is formed into wheels that are four times larger. They are protected with a coating, like a food-grade Elmer's glue, that hardens and slows down the moisture loss in the cheese. Big Sky ages for

---

3   Carey Polis, "25 Most Important Cheeses of America, According to Cheese Experts," Bon Appétit, April 25, 2018, https://www.bonappetit.com/gallery/most-important-chees-es-in-america?srsltid=AfmBOoodIn_5IUa5ig_joqXf7YVzAuJwdTpDlzZoDLQMX9_NBIHFaM5R.

three years, and by that time, it has flavors similar to Parmesan cheese, Lehner says, but it is not a Parmesan.

"I like to tell people it's too good to cook with. Get a good bottle of wine and eat little snippets of that along with the wine while you're making dinner," he says. Willi's partner, Kitas McKnight, likes to grate the Grana over steamed vegetables.

Lehner makes Havarti cheese at Cedar Grove Cheese, using certified organic milk obtained through Cedar Grove. Havarti has extra cream added during production. "That gives you cheese with a more buttery, velvety mouth feel," Willi says. The cultures are different from those used for cheddar, and the Havarti curds are stirred and separated more than those for cheddar, giving the salt more time to be absorbed.

"Our motto is: We don't sell cheap cheese. We sell really good cheese."

THAT COOL AGING CAVE

Bleu Mont's cheese cave opened in 2007. It took a full year to build.

First, there was a massive hole to dig: 14 feet down into a hillside, 85 feet long, and 40 feet wide. The concrete floor was poured, steel I-beams and rebar formed the skeleton structure, and Styrofoam was bent to create arches so that the walls curved around and up like a Quonset hut. Then, concrete was blown onto the structure in several layers and topped with a waterproof covering. "There's 440,000 pounds of concrete and 8,500 rebar ties in the cave," Willi says.

Finally, the cave was covered with 12 feet of soil and limestone rocks that had been excavated from the site and planted with prairie grasses.

"It's the strongest structure. It won't fall and crush the cheese," Lehner says.

Inside, the cave is 66 feet long and 12 feet high where the rounded walls meet at the top of the dome. An entry vestibule with a place to change footwear and a processing room were added later.

As an unexpected side benefit, the acoustics inside the cave are amazing. "In the smaller room, I can sing a note and it sustains long enough that I can harmonize with my own voice," McKnight says.

McKnight also contributed her own good karma to the cave. In the depths of the pre-construction pit, she positioned a huge, clear quartz crystal "to bring good energy." Has it helped? Hard to tell, she says, but adds, "There's a lot of great cheese coming out of that cave."

The cave project came about because Lehner simply ran out of space to age his cheeses. He had started aging the bandaged

cheddar in a small, bathroom-sized space in one of the buildings on the property. With the help of a grant from the now-defunct Wisconsin Dairy Business Innovation Center, Lehner traveled to England, Ireland, and Scotland, visiting cheesemakers and getting advice. "Every single one said to build the cheese cave underground. Mother Earth takes care of the temperature, and being underground also gives us almost the perfect humidity," Lehner says.

When the cheese is fully aged, McKnight cuts the rounds and wraps the wedges in white paper for sale. Bleu Mont is carried in cheese shops and sold to restaurants through distributors in Chicago, Minneapolis, southern California, and New York. Bleu Mont does not market its products online and doesn't even have a website. But Lehner and McKnight sell the cheeses at the Dane County Farmers' Market, with a beautiful, quilted mountain landscape—stitched by Madison fabric artist Cherie St. Cyr—as a backdrop on one side of their booth and a sign on the other end that reads "Stupid good cheese."

LIVING SUSTAINABLY

Aside from making cheese, Lehner is passionate about the environment. A view from the long, oak tree-lined gravel driveway to the home he shares with McKnight reveals solar panels and a 120-foot-tall wind turbine sitting in fields on the property, with more solar panels on top of their home. The solar energy provides hot water and electricity, and along with the wind turbine, Lehner's renewable installation "produces an estimated five times more electricity than we use," he says, sending the excess onto the electric grid.

He has built a greenhouse made from straw bales, plastered with adobe. It's filled with fig trees, citrus trees, jade plants, and red geraniums. The 2024 fig harvest was a bumper crop, producing as many as 500 figs in the indoor garden. "I use them in my green smoothies," Lehner says. The geranium plant, cut from his mother's garden 20 years ago, now measures about three feet high and six feet wide and, somehow, blooms year-round.

Around the house, Katsura trees—a hardwood native to Japan, with heart-shaped leaves and brightly colored flowers—decorate the homestead and exude a perfume-like fragrance. Lehner has planted hundreds of trees since he bought the property 30 years ago.

Way before Willi had any thoughts of creating his own cheese brand, when he was about 19, he went back to his family's homeland in Switzerland, mountaineering with his brother Peter. "We made cheese out in the Alpine pastures, on mountainsides at about a 6,000- to 7,000-foot elevation. It's way labor-intensive, but it's the best cheese on the planet," he says. They cooked the curds and whey in a copper kettle over a wood fire, as it's been done for centuries.

"The cows were only up there for three months. We milked them twice a day. The evening's milking developed a thick layer of cream that we would skim off the next morning. We used the cream to make butter every three or four days. We also made cheese every day.

"I was having a peak experience, and I didn't even realize it at the time," Lehner says. "It made such a big impression on me. I saw the connection between what the cows eat and the final product."

COMING HOME

Switzerland was Lehner's home base for 10 years, but he spent much of the time traveling around Europe, Nepal, India, China, and Tibet. "I am nuts about mountains. And the Himalayas were there." With all of those mountains around, he also grew to love skiing, which became a lifelong hobby, with near-annual trips to Jackson Hole, Wyoming.

What brought Willi back to Wisconsin after years of exploring the world? "In my late 20s, I started to get the bug to have a home, a more permanent place. A property in Blue Mounds came up for sale, and I started working for my dad and experimenting with cheese." Four decades later, the gamble seems to have paid off.

Oh, and the yodeling. That goes back to Willi's childhood. When his parents came to the U.S. in the 1950s, his mother felt homesick for her Swiss culture. Family members in Switzerland sent her recordings of Swiss music.

"She lined us up and had all six of us learn the songs. We became like the singing von Trapps [the family from *The Sound of Music*]. We performed at weddings, anniversaries, Christmas events, and at the Wilhelm Tell and Heidi Festivals in New Glarus. At least, until all of our voices changed."

Willi says he will still yodel when people ask him to, switching back and forth between a normal voice and falsetto.

No wonder *The New York Times* called him a "rock star."[4]

....

Name: Bleu Mont Cheese

Owner: Cheesemaker Willi Lehner

Community: Blue Mounds

Established: 1986

Website: None

Retail shop: None

Email: bleumont@tds.net

Tours: None

....

4   Christine Muhlke, "Push Comes to Chèvre," *New York Times*, March 30, 2008, https://www.nytimes.com/2008/03/30/style/tmagazine/30wisconsin.html.

The dairy industry contributes $52.8 billion to Wisconsin's economy annually, which is comparable to the annual revenue of companies such as Nike and American Airlines. In fact, dairy produces more revenue for Wisconsin than citrus for Florida and potatoes for Idaho combined.

BRUNKOW CHEESE
JOE BURNS

At the Dane County Farmers' Market, the aroma of sizzling cheese rises, beckoning shoppers to taste samples in flavors such as bacon, cranberry, jalapeno pepper, and pizza. Crowds surge toward the tables, spearing squares of the warm cheese with toothpicks, trying to choose a favorite.

The bright, canopied booth is a popular stop at the Saturday market. The booth belongs to Brunkow Cheese, and the samples are of Brun-Uusto, a baked cheese designed to be eaten warm, that has drawn nationwide attention to the rural Lafayette County cheesemaker.

Co-owners Karl and Mary Geissbuhler jockey around the tables, keeping the grills warm and the tasting trays filled.

Brunkow Cheese (pronounced like BRONCO) has been operating for 126 years in Fayette, just outside Darlington.

The creamery opened in 1899 as Brunkow Cheese Co-op, named after the family that donated the land for the building. It was a cooperative venture owned by dairy farmers who realized that producing cheese could add value to their milk. Nearly a century later, in the 1990s, the cheesemakers bought out the farmers.

Brunkow makes a wide variety of cheeses, from flavored cheddars and Monterey Jacks to artisan, small-batch, European-style specialties. But it is probably best known in recent years for its Brun-Uusto.

Brun-Uusto is based on a cheese that originated in Finland called juustoleipa (YOO-sto-LAY-pa), which means bread cheese. Jim Path, a retired cheese expert at the UW Center for Dairy Research, whose family roots are in Lapland, introduced the concept to Wisconsin cheesemakers, and Brunkow jumped on the idea.

COINCIDENTAL CONVERGENCE

Juustoleipa came on the scene right around the time that Joe Burns connected with Brunkow.

A native of Omaha, Nebraska, Burns was living in Chicago, working as a wine buyer for a major company. "I went to Green City Market, Chicago's largest farmers' market, and I saw cheese from Illinois, Michigan, and Indiana but none from Wisconsin. I couldn't get over that. Wisconsin is king of cheese," he says.

Burns thought it was time the popular market had a place to highlight Wisconsin cheeses, and, with his sales background, he volunteered to help with the booth—just for the fun of it. Little did Burns know that his friendly gesture to publicize Wisconsin cheese would change the course of his life.

Through Norm Monsen, now retired dairy expert with the state Department of Agriculture, Trade and Consumer Protection, word of Burns' gracious offer went out to cheesemakers around the state. "Mary [Geissbuhler] was the only one who called me," says Burns. He drove up to meet Karl and Mary at their southwestern Wisconsin cheese plant to see if their products might interest the Chicago market.

"The winding hills and the rolling pasture—coming from Nebraska's flatlands, I had never seen anything like that. I was so floored by the beauty of the Driftless. It attracted me immediately," he says.

Burns had no background in cheesemaking. At the University of Nebraska, he majored in English and philosophy. After he graduated, he helped run a French bistro and wine bar in Omaha's Old Market district. It was at the bistro that he had his first exposure to artisanal cheeses, wines, and breads, and where he learned how to bake sourdough bread—a hobby that became a passion for Joe well before it turned into a trendy way to get through the COVID-19 pandemic.

The Geissbuhlers and co-owner Greg Schulte were starting to experiment with juustoleipa. They would make the cheese, and another company would cut it, bake it, package it, and handle marketing. The baked cheese tasted buttery and formed a toasty, bread-like crust when warmed in the oven or on a griddle.

When Burns tried it, he instantly felt that it could be a winner. "I knew of Halloumi [a Mediterranean cheese that can be grilled or fried]. Bells went off in my head."

Burns joined Brunkow in 2006 and eventually moved to Mineral Point with his wife and their three children. "I fell in love with Wisconsin," he says. In 2023, Joe bought out Schulte and became a co-owner of the cheese business.

BRUN-UUSTO REIGNS

Brunkow put its own spin on the cheese, developed its own product and its own name: Brun-Uusto. With the help of a vendor at the Dane County Farmers' Market, Burns was able to land a booth for Brunkow at Chicago's Green City Market in Lincoln Park.

"We sold it in Chicago at Green City Market and then we quickly expanded to 14 farmers' markets in the Chicago area, and we got a big account with the Whole Foods Midwest region. It went crazy overnight, and it turned the factory to a totally different focus," Burns says. "We were probably one of the first to put it on the map."

Another element that sets Brun-Uusto apart from most other types of cheese is that it has only rennet and no cultures in it. That makes it sweet and rich, with a caramelized crust from being baked, and it can be enhanced with sweet, savory, or spicy flavors. "It's extremely versatile. Kids love it, and it seems to please everybody," Burns says.

In the past, he had a booth for Brunkow at Chicago's Lollapalooza music festival. "We would cut the Brun-Uusto into thirds, skewer it on sticks like kabobs, grill it, and then drizzle it with condiments or flavors. One of them was black rum maple syrup. It was so popular, it was like throwing bread to pigeons."

Cheese experts like Brun-Uusto, too. The original flavor was named best in its class in the 2022 World Championship Cheese Contest, and jalapeno-flavored won the 2022 gold medal and 2024 silver medal at the World Championship Contests.

Brun-Uusto makes up 80 to 90 percent of the cheese that Brunkow manufactures. It is made in 2,000-pound batches, about four days a week.

And it's not only for bite-sized snacking. Brunkow recently started selling Brun-Uusto as a pizza crust. "It's the same recipe but made in 10-inch round, super-thin pizza crusts, like a gluten-free pizza," Burns says.

OLD-WORLD CHEESES

All of Brunkow's cheeses are made with cow's milk purchased from the Lafayette County Co-op, whose members are all Amish dairy farmers in Lafayette County.

"Their cows are out on the pasture in the spring and summer, and indoors during the winter. They practice sustainable, environmentally friendly agriculture and do not use hormones or antibiotics. It is really high-quality milk," Burns says.

The same milk is the basis for Brun-Uusto as well as a wide variety of other cheeses that Brunkow makes. There are cheddars, ranging from fresh curds to 17-year-aged cheddar, Monterey Jacks, and a variety of cheese spreads.

Brunkow also makes raclette, a cheese that originated in the Swiss Alps and is often served melted. Although it is served warm, like Brun-Uusto, the two cheeses are very different, Burns says. "Raclette melts; it can be used in fondue or on toasted baguettes. Brun-Uusto holds its shape and does not melt."

And then there's a slate of newer, artisanal cheeses with shades of old-world European styles. They are sold under a separate label, Fayette Creamery, and made in smaller batches.

Avondale Truckle is an English-style, cloth-bound cheddar, cave-aged for 12 to 18 months, that starts with a buttery flavor and tastes more earthy as it ages.

Little Darling is a cave-aged, natural rind Tomme, a cheese made mainly in the French and Swiss Alps. It is named after the nearby city of Darlington.

Pavé Henri is a soft-ripened, washed-rind cheese that tastes like "fresh milk and hazelnuts, but it has a pungent smell," Burns says. It is somewhat similar to Pont-l'Évêque, a washed-rind cow's milk cheese that's made in Normandy, France.

Snow Bale is a creamy, soft-ripened cheese with a bloomy rind, and it is made like a French Neufchâtel, which is also produced in Normandy and is believed to be one of the oldest types of cheese in France, dating back to the sixth century.

Coeur de Fayette—or Heart of Fayette—is Brunkow's latest addition to the artisan line. It is a bigger, heart-shaped version of the Snow Bale cheese, released in time for Valentine's Day 2025 but available year-round.

Burns says the Pavé is an unusual cheese that only a few people make. "It's fussy and takes a ton of detail. It's made in really small batches by hand." The Pavé is aged for 20 to 40 days in a new aging room at Brunkow's plant.

"We first started making it in 2010 then stopped for a while and revamped the recipe to make it more consistent. We reintroduced the cheese in 2024," Burns says.

Try our... Pavé Henri

$10

PAVÉ HENRI
SOFT-RIPENED CHEESE

AVONDALE TRUCKLE

AVONDALE TRUCKLE

Pave Henri
Trappist Monk style washed rind
Cave aged: 20-60 Days
Young: Rich, tangy and nutty
Mature: Supple, creamy, nutty (hazelnut), and aromatic

Avondale Truckle
Bandaged wrapped artisan cheddar cheese
Cellar aged: 12-18 months
Younge: Round buttery flavor
Mature: Buttery, earthly, and full layered profile
Pairs with: Fruity, full bodied red wines and brown Ales or Stouts.

Fresh Cheese
CURDS

Snow Bale is made in round ring molds and is rotated every day as it ages. Burns says it looks like a snow roller, the cylindrical-shaped snowballs that form naturally from the wind. Coeur de Fayette is made the same way but in larger, heart-shaped ring molds.

Burns says his interest in European cheeses probably began while he was working at the French bistro in Omaha, where wines and cheeses were paired. He also likes traveling around Europe to see what's popular in the markets.

Beyond that, though, he says having a diverse line of unique products is important. "A specialty cheese like Brun-Uusto that everyone likes is accessible and made in larger volumes. Artisanal cheeses are more handcrafted and may be more aimed at cheese connoisseurs."

BRUNKOW'S HISTORY

Brunkow Cheese has about 15 employees, including six cheesemakers. Jerry Soddy is a long-tenured, talented cheesemaker who helps oversee the production room, and Jenn McDonald is plant manager and works with general manager Athena Abraham to keep the whole factory running smoothly.

While Joe Burns has been with Brunkow for nearly 20 years, Karl and Mary Geissbuhler have a much longer history with the company. The Geissbuhler family has operated Brunkow since Karl's grandfather, Fred Geissbuhler, arrived in Wisconsin from Switzerland in the 1920s. Fred was a cheesemaker, and four of his sons followed in his footsteps. Two of them, Rudy and Walter, joined Fred at Brunkow and eventually bought into the business, while the other two sons plied their trade elsewhere.

When Walter left Brunkow, Rudy brought in his son Karl. Then when Rudy retired, Greg Schulte, a local dairy farmer, became a

co-owner until Burns joined the company and later bought him out.

Karl, representing the third generation, is still one of the cheesemakers at Brunkow. His wife, Mary, ran the packaging side of the business until she retired.

Joe says he was lucky to have Karl and Greg teach him the ropes of cheesemaking when he realized it had become his passion. Joe has found that cheesemaking brings out his creativity, like cooking or baking bread.

"I focus, as a cheesemaker, on the really small-batch, artisan cheese that is made entirely by hand. I like the whole process of making cheeses and aging them. I like the attention to detail and the care that it demands," he says.

Burns also runs a sister company to Brunkow that showcases Brunkow cheeses.

Baked Cheese Haus, based in Wisconsin, operates booths at Christmas markets in a dozen cities across the U.S., including New York City and Boston, as well as at festivals, farmers' markets, and special events. Burns serves raclette. "We scrape it onto baguettes and sell it as a sandwich, creamy and melty. It's the perfect holiday cold weather food."

Before Burns joined Brunkow, change was in the works at the cheese plant and in the industry. "The world of cheese was evolving rather quickly. Brunkow was in a spot where it might be left behind, so it was transitioning from commodity cheeses, such as private-label block cheddar, Monterey Jack, and colby, to specialty cheeses. The Dane County Farmers' Market was its main outlet," he says.

Having the cheese plant in the Driftless Area also contributes to Brunkow's success. "The Driftless has such a unique footprint of interesting and diverse artisanal cheesemaking. There are a lot of innovative products being made here. I don't even see it as competition," Burns says.

Name: Brunkow Cheese

Owner: Cheesemakers Karl and Mary Geissbuhler and Joe Burns

Community: Fayette

Established: 1899

Website: brunkowcheeseofwi.com

Retail shop: 17975 County Hwy F, Darlington; open Monday through Friday, 7 a.m. to 3 p.m.

Phone: 608–776–3716

Tours: None

CAPRI CHEESE
FELIX THALHAMMER

Some cheesemakers may feel most comfortable in relative obscurity behind the scenes, tinkering with recipes, shaping curds into cheese rounds, and keeping a watchful eye on them as they age.

Not Felix Thalhammer, owner and cheesemaker for Capri Cheese. He comes alive in front of crowds in Madison at the Dane County Farmers' Market on Saturday mornings and the Northside Farmers' Market on Sunday mornings, hawking his goat's milk and sheep's milk cheeses.

"What we've got here is Heaven on a Stick," Thalhammer tempts a potential customer, offering a sample of a soft white cheese on a wooden craft stick. It's not just hype; the creamy garlic-and-chive-infused, buttery chèvre is actually named Heaven on a Stick.

"And it's pretty soft?" another market-goer asks.

"Well, you just ate it. It IS pretty soft," Thalhammer replies.

Thalhammer peppers his pitch at the market with jokes and puns. "His one-liners are as good as the cheese," says a regular customer.

"I may not be the best cheesemaker on the planet, but I'm probably the best cheese comedian," Thalhammer quips.

Thalhammer got into cheesemaking unexpectedly. It was not because of a family history in cheesemaking or even, necessarily, for a love of cheese. The business began because when Thalhammer's son, Leif, was young, he could not digest cow's milk. A friend suggested goat's milk as an alternative, and Leif thrived.

Thalhammer began collecting goats. He started with two and bred them. By the third year, the family had eight Nubian goats roaming their property, well off the beaten path in Richland County. Thalhammer hand-milked four of the goats to feed his son. Together, the animals could produce up to two gallons of milk each day, "way more than what we needed," Thalhammer says. And as Leif grew older, he needed less and less of the goat's milk.

What to do with the surplus? Make cheese!

But first, Thalhammer had to figure out how to do that.

JACK OF ALL TRADES

Felix Thalhammer grew up in Winterthur, Switzerland, a country known for its fine cheeses, like Emmentaler, Gruyère, and raclette. But that's not where he learned the craft of cheesemaking. "I wish I had!" he says, wistfully. His family was not in the business. Thalhammer's father was a draftsman for a ship engineering company, and his mother was a homemaker.

After serving in the Swiss army for the mandatory four months, Felix apprenticed with IBM in Switzerland where his job was to repair Selectric typewriters, and then he was a technician for a microfilm company, keeping its huge cameras in working order. But there were challenges. "A lot of the manuals were printed in English," says Felix, whose native language was German. "I realized I should know English a lot better. So, I went to England and attended an immersive session at a language school for six weeks. It was my first real experience in an English-speaking country."

With some rudimentary knowledge of English under his belt, Thalhammer decided to travel to the U.S. His destination was Madison, simply because he knew someone who lived here, a friend with whom he'd played basketball. Thalhammer arrived in Madison in 1983 on a student visa and took more English classes at UW–Madison.

Through the UW, Thalhammer found out about a privately-run program (no longer operating) that offered room and board at a farm to people who would help work on the farmstead. He had a hankering for rural life, so he jumped at the opportunity. It took him to the Richland County site, off a two-lane road, and up a long, narrow, unpaved driveway.

The couple who owned the land and lived there were not farmers. They had tried raising sheep but were inexperienced and gave up on that. They lived in an old log home on the property, where Thalhammer joined them, and together, they worked to build a new house. "That's where I learned American construction techniques," Thalhammer says.

A few years later, the owners abandoned their rural dreams and moved to Madison. Thalhammer stayed and eventually bought the property, including an old barn, most of which dates back to 1900.

In the meantime, Thalhammer met and married Catherine Young, a former elementary school teacher and park ranger/naturalist for the National Park System, and now a writer and a poet. The couple settled into their bucolic rural life at the Richland County homesite and had two children.

Felix dabbled with farming, but the land didn't cooperate. "We had 20 tillable acres—not big enough for any normal herd to graze. There's a lot of woodland, some prairie remnants, and wetlands, and it's a two-story farm, running up the ridge."

Ridges abound in the Driftless, so it's not unusual that part of Thalhammer's property is up on a higher plane, accessible by vehicle but not wide enough for heavy-duty equipment, such as large tractors or combines. Goats can manage the incline, but cows would do too much damage.

Instead of farming, Felix and Catherine ran a business called Logs to Lumber. Felix had a portable sawmill that he would transport to clients' homes and saw customized boards from their logs and downed trees. It was a service for people whose projects were too small for the area's sawmills to tackle.

When Catherine and Felix's son, Leif, came along and was lactose intolerant, Felix shifted gears.

LEARNING THE CHEESE CRAFT

The abundance of goat's milk prompted Felix to explore the world of cheesemaking. He took a short course on cheesemaking at UW–Madison. He talked to other cheesemakers, and he visited Swiss Valley Farms in Luana, Iowa, and bought some of their animals. He got good at milking the goats by hand.

"I was as fast as a machine," he says. "I could do each one in about a minute and a half."

Thalhammer started experimenting with cheese techniques in the family's home, using a 25-gallon, stainless-steel, modified soup kettle. "I was home with my son, and Catherine was teaching. Once a week, I would have enough milk to make feta. It was easy to make. The cheesemaker at Luana told me to use the whey for making brine, add salt, and close the buckets well enough to get the air out of them. I realized that's how they did it in Greece."

The cheese tinkering worked so well that in 2000, Thalhammer decided to take the plunge and create his own commercial operation. With the help of a plumber, an electrician, and a neighbor who knew about construction, he spent two years building a small cheese factory—or, as he and Catherine call it, a microcheesery—just a few steps from their home. The building, designed to meet Wisconsin Department of Agriculture, Trade and Consumer Protection requirements, is made of steel and wood, with tiled walls, and contains a room to produce the cheese, a room to store and age it, and a separate room for packaging. Catherine sold cheese subscriptions to family friends to help pay for the new building.

When the cheesery was completed in 2002, Thalhammer founded Capri Cheese.

CAPRI'S LAUNCH

Capri started with 20 goats, and the herd gradually increased organically. By 2005, Felix and Catherine had amassed about 100 goats, 50 of them for milking and the others as potential replacements when the milking goats grew older or got sick.

Once a week, Felix would pasteurize the goat's milk and make cheese under the supervision of a licensed cheesemaker until Thalhammer earned his cheesemaker's license in 2005. At the time, the concept of a homestead goat dairy was still relatively unusual in Wisconsin.

Capri's first product was a goat's milk feta, brined and aged at the homestead microcheesery, and Thalhammer landed a coveted vendor's booth at the Dane County Farmers' Market. Several local restaurateurs were among his early customers, including Odessa Piper, founder of L'Etoile; Willy Street Co-op

CHEESE

You GOTTA HAVE IT!

FRESH CHÈVRE

Plain (A CLASSIC!)
Black Garlic
Butter, Garlic + Chives
Strawberry 🍓
capri

was also a client. Goat's milk was popular in the form of the classic French chèvre, a soft spread, but it was less common to find it turned into feta, a harder cheese.

One of the early goat cheese vendors in the area was Anne Topham of Fantome Farm in Ridgeway. Considered Wisconsin's grande dame of goat cheese, Topham was known for the high-quality chèvre she produced for nearly 30 years. "Anne invited me to her farm. I watched what she did, and I bought at least two of her does. I admired her, and out of respect for her, I didn't want to make my own chèvre and compete with her," Thalhammer says.

Not only was Capri's goat feta unusual, but what really made it special was the milk. Catherine says, "It was our milk, and it was organic. It went straight from the milking parlor to the vat. That was what we had intended with our homestead cheese."

At the peak, in around 2005, Thalhammer was making up to 400 pounds of feta each week—all by himself—packing the cheese into several coolers and driving an hour and 45 minutes to the Saturday market around the Capitol Square. Business was good.

Then in 2008, the Great Recession hit, the most severe crisis to affect the global economy since the Great Depression of the 1930s. Predatory lending to low-income homebuyers had built up a trove of too-risky loans, and the housing bubble burst, taking down financial institutions, slashing investments and retirement accounts, eliminating jobs, and increasing poverty.

For Capri Cheese, it was also a blow. Some stores stopped selling the more expensive artisan cheese labels, and the market shrank. By then, Thalhammer had quit milking his own goats and had started outsourcing milk production from a farm nearby. "It was costing me way more money to produce the milk than to buy it," he says.

He also had started making his cheeses at the Cedar Grove Cheese plant in Plain and at other area cheese plants to accommodate the higher volume. Before long, though, goat's milk became hard to buy, so Thalhammer supplemented with sheep's milk and expanded his repertoire. He experimented with sheep's milk feta and gouda, adding different flavorings. And he saw that local cheese factories were making cheddar all the time, so he also learned to make cheddar. Noticing that consumers were looking for stronger flavors, he began aging some of his cheeses. "This is quite the thing now," Thalhammer says. "People want aged cheese, AND they want fresh cheese."

Then COVID-19 hit in 2020. The Dane County Farmers' Market suspended its weekly live event over concerns about the thousands of shoppers parading in tight clusters around the Capitol Square. Instead, customers ordered online and picked up their prepackaged, prepaid products by driving through a barn at the Expo Center and stopping at well-spaced vendor tables.

Thalhammer could not lure consumers in person with his cheese samples and his jokes. So, he began vending his products at the Northside Farmers' Market, which continued operating during the pandemic. It was a time to broaden his resources.

CHEESE VARIETY

Today, Thalhammer makes goat's milk feta, cheddar, and creamy chèvre, and sheep's milk gouda, cheddar, and feta—each in several flavors and ages—and about every six weeks, he makes a batch of fresh goat's milk cheddar curds.

Thalhammer manufactures his cheese at Cedar Grove, then ages and packages it in his cheesery.

Around the homestead, seven purebred Nubian goats still hold court, but they are pets, not for milking. Six chickens also strut around the property, with a lone rooster sticking close behind. The farm remains a quirky patchwork of fields and tree groves along a sloping hillside, with weeping willow branches extending over the narrow, still-unpaved driveway.

It reflects the nature of the Driftless, with curvy hills, spaghetti-thin roads and streams, and an often unexpected mixture of trees and prairie.

As part of the inherent respect for nature, Capri's cheesery is equipped with solar panels that began producing electricity in September 2024. An older set of solar collectors on the family's home has been providing hot water since the late 1980s. "I think it is important to be sustainable and try to treat the Earth right," Thalhammer says.

At the market, Heaven on a Stick is one of Capri's best sellers. The goat cheese is mixed with a small amount of butter from Viroqua-based Organic Valley. "It was an experiment. It just tasted really good that way," Thalhammer said. "I brought it to the market and asked people if they liked it; you can get immediate feedback. And the name came when a customer gave it that description."

At the final fall Northside market in October 2024, buyers were snapping up containers of chèvre and packages of hard cheese to store over the coming months. The soft spreads can be frozen, but Thalhammer cautioned, "Don't freeze the hard cheeses. Their structure will change, and they will be more crumbly. They'll be okay for cooking, though."

One enthusiastic buyer took home more than $90 worth of cheese, Thalhammer said.

A new customer said she only eats goat cheese and dropped a package into her basket. "It's good for your stomach,"

Thalhammer agreed. Straight-faced, he added, "If you die, you can always bring it back for a full refund."

Capri cheeses pair well with wine. He says, the stronger cheeses will want a more robust flavor profile, like heavier reds and pinot noir; the milder, younger cheeses need a lighter touch, such as sauvignon blanc or a German Riesling.

Thalhammer sells Capri cheese year-round at the Dane County Farmers' Market, on the Capitol Square from mid-April through early November, at Monona Terrace through December, and at the Garver Feed Mill until mid-April.

Felix also has a side gig, leading occasional tours of Switzerland. "It's a unique vacation destination, with the Alps, the lakes, good bike riding, and a great train system that is on time," he says. "They also make outstanding cheese."

The tours are arranged at the request of customers, and they are custom-designed to cover whatever the customers want to see and do. And yes, cheese is generally one of the highlights of the itinerary. Certain cheese factories across Switzerland offer tours, where visitors can view the cheesemaking through glass-enclosed areas and then sample the products. "That's a big part of the trips," Thalhammer says.

Another big part for Thalhammer is riding his bicycle in the Alps. Cycling is one of his hobbies, sometimes for four- or five-hour rides through Wisconsin's countryside. "I ride fast—that's where you get the exercise. It's liberating, and it makes you appreciate where we live in the Driftless," he says. Navigating the region's hills also prepares him for riding in the Alps.

When Thalhammer is back in Switzerland, "the familiar language and landscape that I knew as a child bring back memories."

But the Driftless is Thalhammer's home now. "It has a really interesting landscape. It's a beautiful place with really good energy—a real earth-preserving place," he says. "You can't duplicate that."

....

Name: Capri Cheese

Owner: Cheesemaker Felix Thalhammer

Community: Blue River

Established: 2002

Website: Not active

Retail shop: None

Phone number: 608–604–2640

Email: felix@capricheese.com

Tours: None

....

Wisconsin is the number one dairy goat
state in the U.S.

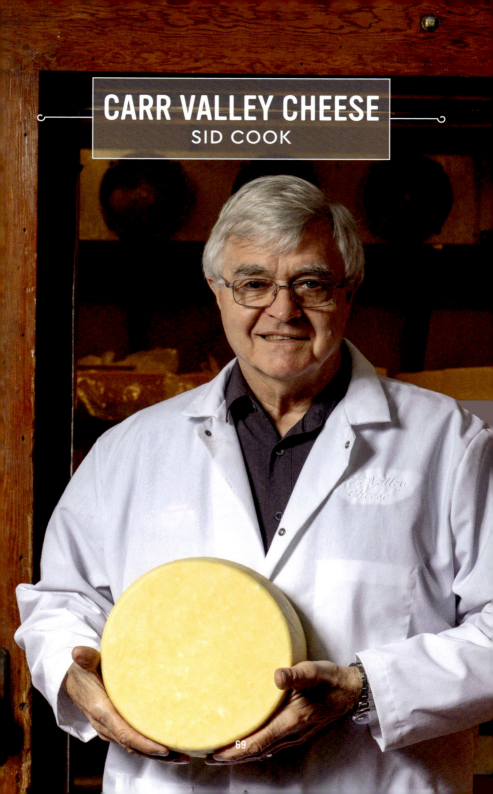

CARR VALLEY CHEESE
SID COOK

Sid Cook is the elder statesman of cheesemaking in the Driftless Area. He has had a hand in making cheese—literally—for 60 years.

A Wisconsin Master Cheesemaker and owner of Carr Valley Cheese, Cook is a fourth-generation cheesemaker; his family has been in the business for nearly a century and a half. "I'm from a tribe of cheesemakers," he says.

Cook's great-great uncle, Ed Lepley, was the first. In 1883, Lepley ran the Springdale cheese plant just north of Viola, a town that straddles Richland and Vernon Counties in southwest Wisconsin. Sid's grandparents, his parents, and other relatives carried on the tradition and owned cheese plants in small communities throughout the Driftless region.

Every other Sunday, the family would gather at his grandmother's house in La Farge, and the conversation centered around one topic. "They would get together and talk about cheese—what starter worked best, who they were selling cheese to, which warehouse was paying more. I grew up with that," he says.

Sid's parents' cheese factory, Irish Valley, was right next door to the family's home in Plain, in Sauk County—sort of an extension of their home.

"Every morning at breakfast, I would open the kitchen door and the milk trucks were unloading milk into the vats. Dad would weigh the milk and write, in pencil, the date and weight of milk delivered from each farm." The trucks came seven days a week, and Sid's father made cheese seven days a week.

As a young child, Sid spent a lot of time in the factory, driving a tricycle or a tractor around the vats.

Irish Valley was the type of place where customers could walk right into the plant, step past the vats where cheese was being made, and buy a chunk of cheese. "They would take customers in back, into the cooler, cut off a hunk of the cheese they wanted to buy, wrap it in white paper, and sell it. If they were too busy making cheese, customers would just have to wait," Cook says.

Sid started making his own vats of cheese at Irish Valley when he was 12 years old and earned his cheesemaker's license when he was 16. But following in his family's footsteps was not always part of his life plan. He got a bachelor's degree in political science from the University of Wisconsin–Platteville, thinking he might work toward a career as an attorney.

"Then I thought, *Hmm, do I really want to sit behind a desk for the rest of my life?* So I went into the family business, and damn if I didn't end up sitting behind a desk anyway," he says.

A CORNUCOPIA OF CHEESES

After working at his parents' Irish Valley cheese plant and later owning it for a while, Cook bought his first Carr Valley Cheese factory in 1986. Carr Valley doesn't date quite as far back as Cook's family history in the cheese industry, but it's not far behind; its roots go back to 1902.

Over the years, Cook has greatly expanded Carr Valley's capacity and its output, and he now heads a small empire of artisan cheese production that's based primarily in La Valle, a village in Sauk County with a population of less than 400, about 20 miles west of Wisconsin Dells.

Carr Valley makes more than 100 types of dairy products using cow's, goat's, and sheep's milk. They include some uncommon offerings such as beer cheddar; black truffle goat cheese; Cocoa Cardona, a goat cheese rubbed with cocoa powder; and Airco, a semisoft, smoked cheese made from a combination of cow's, goat's, and sheep's milk. There are also bread cheeses, curds, and specialty butters.

"We're really proud of what we do," Cook says. "We've made a lot of really good cheeses, and we've won more than 1,000 national and international awards over the years."

Carr Valley has about 140 full-time and part-time employees and produces about 70,000 or 80,000 pounds of dairy products a week. That amounts to nearly four million pounds a year. Most of the milk comes from local dairy farms and co-ops, all within about 25 miles of La Valle. Some are second- or third-generation dairy farms that are long-time suppliers to Carr Valley.

"We have a waiting list of farms [interested in working with Carr Valley]. We balance our milk and buy some from farms and the rest from co-ops," Cook says.

GROWING THE BUSINESS

When Cook bought the Carr Valley Cheese plant in La Valle in 1986, the factory was producing 23-pound, wrapped cheddar wheels, aged 30 to 90 days, and waxed. Most were sold to a company that distributed the cheese to family-owned grocery stores with no refrigeration in rural areas of the South. "The cheese had to be very high quality to survive the high temperatures. The stores would have a cutter with a big blade, and they would cut wedges for customers. They called it hoop cheese," Cook says.

The Mauston plant was added in 1991 after the previous owners filed for bankruptcy. Fennimore came on board in around 2006 when the owner wanted to retire. Then in 2010, when the owners of the Linden factory wanted to sell, Cook purchased the plant, which already was making Carr Valley's blue cheese.

Today, the main plant at La Valle makes vat-salted cheeses such as colby, Monterey Jack, and artisan bandaged cheddar.

The Mauston plant makes all of the butters and the brine-salted cheeses, such as baby Swiss, gouda, fontina, Mobay, and Cardona.

Fennimore is the home of the bread cheese production. Butters are also packaged there.

The Linden facility is still producing blue cheeses; their process calls for dry salting.

Will there be more cheese factories added to the lineup? "Absolutely not," Cook replies. And then, after a couple of moments, he adds, "But you never know."

In addition to the factories, Carr Valley has a facility in Portage where the cheese is aged, cut, and packaged; a sales and marketing office in Baraboo; and seven retail cheese stores around the region.

Traveling among them can get to be time-consuming. "A lot of times, my car is my office," Cook says.

GROWING UP IN THE DRIFTLESS

Like his company's cheese, Cook is a product of the Driftless Area. He grew up there and has always lived in the region.

"I grew up out in the country, between Plain and Leland. There were incredible sandstone outcroppings in the area," he says. "My friends and I would run around down in the marsh or creek or up in the hills. I lived three miles from Natural Bridge State Park, and we would go out in the fields and look for arrowheads. Once, I found an arrowhead in a neighbor's yard near a tree. One kid found a mammoth tooth in a field and brought it to school to show everyone. It gives you a sense of the history of the area," he says.

The topography and geology of the region also have an impact on the cheese industry. Producing cheese in the Driftless gives it a distinctive flavor, with more fruity or floral notes that intensify as the cheese ages, Cook says.

"In New York or Vermont, the cheddar has more sulphury notes than ours, and on the West Coast, the cheese tastes more grassy.

"It's really about what the cows are eating. The pastures we have here in the Driftless really have a lot to do with terroir. If you look at a map of Wisconsin, we have the Mississippi River, Lake Michigan, and Lake Superior—about 14 percent of the world's freshwater is in Lake Superior alone. And there are the Wisconsin and Fox Rivers.

"We have a tremendous water supply here, which makes our grasses grow, and we have a vast variety of plants sitting on the edge of the water," Cook says.

INNOVATING WITH FLAVORS

Cheesemaking is a hard job, but even after six decades in the business, Cook takes pleasure in his life's work. "I love cheese. I love making new products that other people haven't done before. Developing new flavors and coming up with names for them—it's very exciting to do that, and then we take them to the market and sell them," he says.

Consumers' tastes have also changed, which helps broaden the spectrum of cheese possibilities. "I used to make cheddar, colby, Monterey Jack, brick, and Swiss. I think most people grew up on processed American cheese or mild cheddar. Today, I make cheeses with flavors, and with names such as Gran Canaria, Mobay, and Cardona."

Gran Canaria is named for the Canary Islands, where Cook tried a mixed milk cheese on a cruise. "The waiter's grandmother made it. He wasn't supposed to let me taste it, but I had brought some of our cheese along, so we tasted each other's." The grandmother's cheese had been marinated in olive oil, so Cook decided to try that, too.

The result, Gran Canaria, is made with sheep's, cow's, and goat's milk. The cheese wheels are coated with olive oil and aged for at least two years. "There's a sweet, citrusy taste from the sheep's milk on the front of your tongue, a cow's milk taste on the palate, and if you breathe through your nose, just a tad of a goat's milk note. And a bit of a smell of olives," Cook says.

Mobay is a semi-hard cheese with three parts pressed together, sandwich style: one section is made from goat's milk, one from sheep's milk, and between them is a layer of ash, creating three flavor profiles, Cook says. Originally, the ash was from grapevines; now, it's a pharmaceutical-grade vegetable ash.

Cardona is a semi-hard goat cheese aged for eight months, and it comes in a variety of flavors. The Cocoa Cardona is rubbed with cocoa powder. Where did that idea come from? "I've eaten chocolate and cheese together for years," Cook says. "In our stores, we carry a chocolate cheese with nuts [made by another company]. I would take a piece of cheddar and make a sandwich with the chocolate cheese. They really go well together.

"A nice dark chocolate and blue cheese is really, really good, and Swiss or aged cheddar go with chocolate, too. The acidity of the cheese and the sweetness of the chocolate—what's not to like?"

Cook has earned Wisconsin Master Cheesemaker certification for cheddar, fontina, Gran Canaria, and Mobay.

DEALING WITH REGULATIONS

The dairy industry, overall, has changed over the years, Cook says.

For one thing, cheese production is much more expensive, with higher costs for milk, labor, supplies, packaging, and transportation.

Another factor is the numerous rules Wisconsin and the federal government have imposed on cheese and cheesemaking. Not only is Wisconsin the only state in the nation to require cheesemakers to be licensed, but others involved in the process must also obtain licenses.

Cook says that when he started working in the business at age 14, he could haul milk to the plant without a special license or even a driver's license. One farm was 200 feet down the road; another was 400 feet away in the other direction. "Dad would say, 'Get in the milk truck and pick up Wilhelm's milk.' Today, you need a sampler's license to do that. You have to hire someone to pick up milk in a milk truck, and under federal law, they need a commercial driver's license to drive that truck. You pay them about $5,000 to go to school for six months, plus salary, to drive a milk truck."

The sampler's license is a state requirement. The driver has to measure how much milk is in the truck, stir it, and put a sample on ice in the back of the truck. Under Wisconsin law, they have to go back to school for testing every two years.

In the 1970s, the state required dairy plants that had been heat-treating their milk to fully pasteurize it instead. Many small cheese plants closed because they couldn't afford the $70,000 cost of a pasteurizer, Cook says.

There are a lot of inspections and paperwork requirements, too. "You have to run tests for E. coli, listeria, and coliform. We have our own labs for testing, but when you sell a product, many companies are required to get audits by third parties. That can involve compiling 30 to 40 pages of background information every time we have a new customer. And new regulations are on the way related to product recalls.

"It's a lot. It makes it very difficult for small cheese companies," Cook says.

NATIONAL ATTENTION

Carr Valley's Glacier Point Gorgonzola was featured on Bravo's *Top Chef: Wisconsin* series, used by Chef Kenny Nguyen in a crab rangoon salad. The dish didn't win, but the experience was still "great," Cook says.

"I had a second of glory twice—they flash your picture up for a second or two. It was fun to be part of it. And it was shocking how secretive they were about everything," he says.

Sid and his cheeses have also had other flashes of national notoriety. Among them, a *Wine Spectator* article in 2024 called Cook "Wisconsin's master of invention,"[1] and a *Wall Street Journal* feature in 2012 called Cook "The reigning whiz of artisanal cheese."[2]

Carr Valley cheeses are sold around the U.S. and in several other countries, such as Australia, Austria, Kuwait, and Hong Kong. Many of those customers are hotels or Americans living abroad, Cook says.

FAVORITES

So, with all of those cheese varieties and flavors, does Cook have a favorite or two?

"I'm a real fan of aged cheddar," he says. One of his favorite ways to eat it is with potatoes. Cook's family makes a cheese-and-potato dish that's a highlight of every Christmas, Thanksgiving, and Easter. Similar to au gratin potatoes, it consists of several layers of thinly sliced potatoes, roux, and shredded cheddar.

Another tradition of Cook's involves a combination of cheeses. "I love making fondue with whatever cheeses are left over, like

---

1 David Gibbons, "Wisconsin's Master of Invention," *Wine Spectator*, April 30, 2024, https://www.winespectator.com/articles/wisconsin-cheese-carr-valley-sid-cook-043024.

2 J.S. Marcus, "The Reigning Whiz of Artisanal Cheese," The *Wisconsin State Journal*, January 7, 2012, https://www.wsj.com/articles/SB10001424052970203462304577138711225918048.

fontina, Emmental, Marisa, or Cardona, and dipping French bread with a hard crust into it." To elevate his fondue, he rubs the fondue pot with cut garlic before putting the cheese in, and adds white wine or kirsch, a cherry-flavored brandy, to the cheese mixture.

"A Swiss watchmaker taught me how to do this in Switzerland. We would have a shot of kirsch with the fondue or drink the same wine you use in the fondue. It was an education," Cook says.

One of Cook's favorite cheeses is Marisa, a semi-hard sheep's milk cheese that's named after his daughter. Originally made with a thistle coagulate from Spain, the cheese had a "little bitterness from the thistle, a bit immature and prickly." Later, the recipe for the cheese was tweaked, and regular rennet was used instead of the thistle. "It aged out nicely," Cook says.

Cook and his team at Carr Valley are always dreaming up new cheese variations. What's coming next? "A cured brick. It's a really nice cheese, and we're working on a cheese that has the taste of Parmesan but in a smaller wheel."

Asked if a fifth or sixth generation of his family will continue to shepherd the cheese business, Cook says, "Some of the kids are working in the organization; we'll see how that all goes."

In the meantime, Cook has no regrets about his own career choice. "It's been a great run. I've always really enjoyed making cheese; it's been a joy to be able to make so many different cheeses. It's never really seemed like a job. I've been lucky to be able to do that."

....

Name: Carr Valley Cheese

Owner: Wisconsin Master Cheesemaker Sid Cook

Community: La Valle

Established: 1902

Website: carrvalleycheese.com

Retail shops: La Valle, Fennimore, Mazomanie, Sauk City, Wisconsin Dells, and two in Mauston

Phone: 800-462-7258

Tours: None, but at Mauston and La Valle, visitors can view cheesemaking through a window, if they arrive early.

....

Wisconsin is home to about 5,300 dairy farms—more than any other state—and 99 percent are family-owned, according to Dairy Farmers of Wisconsin, which tracks dairy cows.

CEDAR GROVE CHEESE
BOB WILLS

Cedar Grove Cheese, in Plain, may have been the first cheese plant in the Driftless region, and for that, it holds a special place in the area's history.

But what owner and Wisconsin Master Cheesemaker Bob Wills hangs his hat on is not the past, but the future. His cheesemaking philosophy is intimately tied to health, the environment, and a sense of community, empowering farmers and the new generations of cheesemakers. Innovation is woven into the fabric of Cedar Grove.

Cedar Grove cheese comes from cows that have never been given synthetic growth hormones. Wills says his plant was the first in the country to take that position, starting in 1993, at the behest of both farmers and customers of Cedar Grove.

Located on a quiet, side road about 10 miles north of Spring Green in Sauk County, the cheese plant probably boasts the most unusual and most attractive wastewater treatment facility of any cheesemaking factory in the country.

Wills also has made it a point to use Cedar Grove as an opportunity to help others in the industry. He has served as mentor to several of the area's newer cheesemakers, such as Anna Landmark of Landmark Creamery, and he's allowed other small cheesemakers, including Felix Thalhammer of Capri Cheese, Willi Lehner of Bleu Mont Dairy, and Al Bekkum of Nordic Creamery, to use part of his facility's production space to create their own products.

"I feel like they're family. When I go to a cheese show and see these people, they're raking in awards, sometimes surpassing us. There's always a sense of pride that we played some role in helping them get going and making that possible," Wills says.

CAREER PIVOT

Bob Wills doesn't have cheesemaking in his blood. He grew up in the Milwaukee area, in suburban Brookfield. His father, Robert, was editor and publisher of the *Milwaukee Sentinel*. Bob earned a PhD in economics and a law degree. While he was in college, he worked for Gaylord Nelson, former Wisconsin governor, U.S. senator, and the founder of Earth Day.

Wills was well into a career as an agricultural economist for the University of Wisconsin–Madison and the U.S. Department of Agriculture when Cedar Grove's owner, Ferdie Nachreiner—his father-in-law at the time and owner of the plant since 1947—was about to retire. Wills bought the plant in 1989 and moved his family from urban Madison to very rural Plain. He was stunned by the beauty of the Driftless Area. "They could have turned all of Sauk County into a national park," he says.

The challenge was clear, though. Wills had to learn how to make cheese. That's where Nachreiner and Dan Hetzel, Cedar Grove's lead cheesemaker and former co-owner, helped with the transition. "They taught me the art of cheesemaking. They had very different styles but a strict commitment to the fundamentals of making safe and high-quality cheese." He also took classes through organizations such as the UW Center for Dairy Research to learn more about the science of cheesemaking.

Wills is now a Master Cheesemaker and reigns over a playlist of dozens of cheeses. How many? "Too many. I have no idea," he says. There are cheddars, colbys, and Monterey Jacks, as well as pecorino, Butterkäse, Havarti, and more. Some are made with cow's milk, while others use sheep's or goat's milk or a mixture of milks.

One of his favorites is Weird Sisters, a semisoft, medium-bodied cheese made from a mixture of cow's milk and water buffalo's milk. The buffalo's milk came from an Israeli immigrant who raised the animals on a nearby farm, and later, from another farm, farther north.

"The buffalo's milk was clean and 'milky' sweet. It has very high levels of both butterfat and protein, creating a rich cheese ... As it aged, it gained an earthy character," Wills says. It was named after the witches in Macbeth and the rock band in the Harry Potter series. "The cheese was fabulous. It was the easiest cheese to sell ever, and it won awards," Wills says. "It could be grated on a salad, but really deserved to just be eaten neat, or maybe with an apple." But the water buffalo's milk was only available for about five years. "We couldn't get anybody to milk water buffalo anymore ... I keep hoping someone else will give it a go. We would love to revive the cheese."

Shakespeare characters also show up in the names of other Cedar Grove cheeses, such as Montague, an aged sheep's and cow's milk blend. It's a nod to the nearby American Players Theatre in Spring Green, which includes several of Shakespeare's plays in each season's roster. Donatello, made solely of sheep's milk, is the counterpart to Montague, bringing *Teenage Mutant Ninja Turtles* into the lineup. It's also the name of an Italian Renaissance sculptor.

One of the most popular cheeses that Cedar Grove makes now is in the style of a Brazilian cheese, queijo-de-coalho, that's meant to be cooked on a grill. "If you're sitting on a beach in Brazil, someone will put this cheese on a skewer and grill it on a hibachi; it browns, but it doesn't melt. When I heard about it,

I thought, *This is tailgate cheese. It's the most Wisconsin cheese I've ever heard of*," Wills says.

Cedar Grove's version is called Chees-E-Que, and true to a Wisconsin tailgate, one of the flavors it comes in is bratwurst. "It's a vegetarian sausage made of cheese," says Wills. He sought out Straka Meats, also in Plain, for tips on the spice combination. "We submitted it to a cheese contest, and it got the only perfect score I've ever received in a national competition. Now, we're making 25,000 pounds a week of it. It's at least one-fourth of our production."

WORKING WITH FARMERS

Cedar Grove's roots date back to 1878. It's believed to be the oldest cheese company in the Driftless region, Wills says. The original building probably sat across the road from the current building, which was constructed in about 1900.

Today, the plant makes cheese five days a week, sometimes around the clock, producing about 13,000 pounds each day. The milk comes from 28 farms, including nine that are organic, all a short drive within the Driftless.

"In flat, eastern Wisconsin, it makes sense to have bigger farms and row crops such as corn and beans. In the Driftless, because farms are on hills, the farms tend to be smaller. We specialize in matching with small farmers. A lot more farmers graze their animals on the hillsides, and grass-based milk makes better tasting cheese, and it's healthier for people to eat.

"I could get all of the milk off one farm, but it would make me vulnerable," he says. "It would also defeat our objective to support smaller farmers who, in some cases, might not have an alternative market."

All of the farmers agree with Wills's commitment not to use rBGH, bovine growth hormone, on their cows to increase milk production. Cedar Grove also has pledged not to use cultures or enzymes with genetically modified organisms.

"We are working with farmers who graze their cows on grass, who create buffer strips along streams, build areas to support butterflies, and use cover crops to reduce nutrient runoff and build up the quality of the soil," Wills says.

CLOCK SHADOW CREAMERY

Wills wanted to help farmers close to urban areas, too. That was one reason he opened Clock Shadow Creamery in Milwaukee in 2012, near the Allen-Bradley Clock Tower.

"Part of my motivation was nostalgic. There had never been a cheese factory in the city of Milwaukee, and I thought that was weird. I was also trying to find ways to get more value for the product for farmers on the urban fringe," Wills says. The cheese plant was in a building that won awards for its sustainable design in the historic Walker's Point neighborhood. The area had seen better days when Cedar Grove opened there, but since then, other businesses have invested in the neighborhood, including restaurants and bars. "I felt good about our role in that," Wills says.

The location in the heart of Milwaukee also offered a new perspective to Wills. "One of the things about the Driftless— we're kind of in the middle of nowhere, with a relatively small amount of traffic. In Milwaukee, you're in direct contact with customers, including local restaurants, so we got more feedback, quickly, on products we were developing."

After 11 years, though, Wills decided that commuting between two cheese plants, in Milwaukee and Plain, had become too difficult. In late 2023, he turned over Clock Shadow to Ron and Josie Henningfeld. Ron had been a cheesemaker for Cedar Grove and Clock Shadow, and then he and his wife, Josie, had begun making their own Hill Valley Dairy cheese at the Milwaukee cheese plant.

Cedar Grove's Plain plant still makes some of Clock Shadow's products, including a double-cream colby, Quark, and cheese curds in a larger, more symmetrical shape that restaurants have preferred for deep frying.

Quark is a traditional northern and eastern European style of cream cheese. "When we opened Clock Shadow Creamery, we had requests to make Quark from customers with German, Polish, and Dutch heritage. The cheese is tart, acidic, or lemony," Wills says. It's a versatile cheese that can be used in many ways, from soups to bagel schmears. "My favorite, which was commercially unviable, was brandy old-fashioned Quark made with Korbel, orange, and mulled cherries. My kids used to complain that I would sneak Quark into everything."

EMPLOYEES MATTER

At the plant in Plain—one of the Driftless's bigger artisan operations—there is generally cheesemaking in progress in three vats at any point in time, and little automation is involved. "We're still a factory that's pretty much manual. We have open vats and we hand-cheddar the cheese, like most of the companies in the Driftless." Wills is one of six licensed cheesemakers, and many of the company's 25 employees are immigrants.

"They are from Nicaragua, Mexico, and the Dominican Republic. They are a dependable workforce. They want to be here, they work hard, they are smart, and they are fun. If it weren't for immigrants, we would be out of business," Wills says.

State historical figures show that Wisconsin peaked at 180,000 dairy farms in 1934;[1] now there are 5,300, according to the Dairy Farmers of Wisconsin.[2] "We lost so many dairy farmers, and because of that, we lost so much of the labor supply. And rural communities hollowed out. In Plain, we lost our grocery store, bowling alley, feed mill, hardware store, daycare center,

1   Number of monthly milk cow herds, Wisconsin, 2004 to Current, https://www.nass.usda.gov/Statistics_by_State/Wisconsin/Publications/Dairy/Historical_Data_Series/herd_brt_2004.pdf.

2   Census of Agriculture—Wisconsin, https://agcensus.library.cornell.edu/wp-content/uploads/1940-Wisconsin-COUNTY_TABLES-1265-Table-04.pdf.

and even a bar. All of those are gone, and that's happened all over Wisconsin. If we don't have employees to replace people on farms and working in cheese factories, we need immigrants. They're the ones willing to do the work, and they get excited about it," says Wills.

EMBRACING NEW IDEAS

Innovation is high on the list for Bob Wills. "People don't understand that most innovation comes out of small companies," he says. "We were one of the first to use bulk tanks to transport

milk. We were the first company in Wisconsin to switch to electronic pasteurizer controls instead of pen and paper."

New technology is also playing a role. "We are working on a project to trace milk from the farm it came from to the end product. We will be coming out with organic curds, where if you take a photo of the QR code, it will tell you which farms' milk was used to make the curd and when it came out of the vat, and there will be a link to the farms involved. It's a way to educate consumers about farm practices and to encourage and reward farmers whose practices consumers support," Wills says.

Another key example of Cedar Grove's innovation is its wastewater treatment system, which looks more like a greenhouse than an industrial sanitation facility. The system—built in 1999 and named Living Machine—is located in a building adjacent to the cheese plant. Ten tanks are hooked together, and as the wastewater from the cheese plant runs through each tank, the water gets progressively cleaner.

Here's what else makes the system unique: The tops of the circular tanks are open, and big plants sprout from many of them. The front of the building is a wall of windows, letting the sun in, and the rear wall is covered with a colorful mural painted by Wills's son, Owen, an artist who has also painted murals on skyscrapers in New York. The artwork depicts the way the factory looked to Bob when he got up at sunrise.

"The hills are partly enshrouded in fog, and steam is being blown off the boiler. Further down the mural is a farmer carrying cans of milk. It is a tribute to Lemuel Cooper, who first built the cheese factory in 1878 and brought in a Swiss cheesemaker to help support the new dairy industry in southwest Wisconsin," Bob says. "I asked Owen to include the obligatory cow to which we owe our livelihood, and a sandhill crane exemplifying our commitment to our natural environment."

The idea of Living Machine is to mimic the steps that a wetland would take, but at an accelerated pace, Wills says.

"We provide oxygen and microbes to break down the wastewater, and plants pull some of those nutrients out of the water to help them grow."

A PALETTE OF POSSIBILITIES

Another type of innovation involves cooking up new types of cheese. "That's part of the joy of the job. It's very creative," Wills says. The tools used to create different cheeses, such as enzymes and molds, are ever-changing.

"There used to be a bulk culture, and we would use it for all of our cheeses. Now, we have freeze-dried and frozen cultures that we can purchase, and they are becoming more and more customizable. We can mix and match them. It's like a whole array of paint in a hardware store. It's like an artist getting new colors.

And the public's taste in cheese has broadened, he says. "The other reason we are able to develop new varieties is that the public has become more sophisticated and curious. They come in and ask, 'What's the new thing?' Their sense of adventure and thrill at learning supports product development … and makes the business more fun."

Wills says it's encouraging to see that people are beginning to recognize that there's a group of producers in the Driftless region who are making "unique, really high-quality cheeses, and they're getting a national reputation for it." They are generally small operations, with hands-on attention to detail, getting milk from farmers connected to the land.

"Milk isn't just generic; it has a sense of place," he says. "The character of our cheeses reflects the nature of the Driftless."

Wills reflects on his career with a sense of satisfaction. A former academic, he's never really quit a world of education and research; he's just grown into it in a different way. "In 36 years of working here, I've never had a day that I didn't learn something."

Name: Cedar Grove Cheese

Owner: Wisconsin Master Cheesemaker Bob Wills

Community: Plain

Established: 1878

Website: cedargrovecheese.com

Retail shop: E5904 Mill Rd., Plain,
open Monday through Saturday, 9 a.m. to 3 p.m.
Beginning April 1, store hours are 9 a.m. to 4 p.m.

Phone: 608–546–5284

Tours/other public events: Tours available, generally mornings

More than one-fourth (27 percent) of the cheese made in Wisconsin in 2023 was specialty cheese, totaling 942 million pounds—also the highest of any state.

BEAR VALLEY AFFINAGE

JENIFER BROZAK

Out in the very rural parts of Richland County, there is a small, fairly anonymous-looking, but quite important business for the cheesemakers in the Driftless.

It is Bear Valley Affinage, a place where artisan cheese sits patiently and ages. The word *affinage* (ah-fee-NAHJ) is French; literally, it translates as "to refine." In the cheese business, affinage is the process of caring for cheese as it cures.

At Bear Valley Affinage, there are racks and racks of cheeses stacked in six rooms with different temperature and humidity settings—43 to 52 degrees, with humidity ranging from 60 to 95 percent—depending on what the cheeses need to thrive. Some of the cheeses are made with cow's milk, others with sheep's or goat's milk, and still others, a mixture of milks. Each is developing a distinct flavor and texture as it ages.

The cheeses are quietly maturing under the watchful eye of Jenifer Brozak. She is an *affineur*, a person who practices the art of affinage.

"My job is comparable to being the finish carpenter on fancy home remodeling projects," she says.

INSIDE THE AFFINAGE

The concrete block building that houses Bear Valley Affinage is about 75 years old. (The cooler, added later, is only about 50 years old.) It is in Bear Valley, an unincorporated community about 13 miles east of Richland Center, that consists mainly of a handful of businesses clustered on about two blocks of

Highway 130. The building once housed a cheese factory where local farmers brought their milk, and the factory owner lived upstairs, which was common then.

On a rare visit by outsiders to the affinage last fall, Brozak led the guests through a metal door to access the cooling rooms where the cheeses are housed. "They're all sleeping here," she said, with a grin.

A native of rural Richland County, Brozak had worked at Cedar Grove Cheese in Plain, and at Meister Cheese in Muscoda, managing customized artisan cheese orders for clients.

In 2010, she decided to branch off on her own. The affinage now handles cheeses from Cedar Grove, Carr Valley, and Brunkow—about 60,000 pounds of cheese each year.

"Jenifer is a skilled affineur. We have worked with her on different projects for many years," says Sid Cook, owner and Wisconsin Master Cheesemaker at Carr Valley Cheese.

THE ART OF AGING

Affinage is more than just a waiting game; it is active manipulation of the exterior of the cheese and control over the conditions of the aging cave. Depending on the type of cheese, the rounds or blocks often have to be brushed with a brine or other culture solution, coated, salted, pierced, and/or turned according to a specific schedule, all while the temperature and humidity in the room are closely supervised. These key elements in the process allow the cheese to mature to its desired texture and flavor.

Supervising the cheeses is a big responsibility. Brozak says, "Oh, absolutely! I fully intend to turn out the best cheese I can possibly turn out.

"With cheese, consistency is a big thing. People don't want a cheddar that tastes different each time they buy it. And these are expensive cheeses, so there's more pressure to make it as consistent as possible."

LEARNING AFFINAGE

You may wonder how one learns to be an affineur, a very specialized and critical aspect of cheesemaking.

"Trial and error," Brozak says. It started with encouragement from Cedar Grove owner and Wisconsin Master Cheesemaker

Bob Wills. When a coworker at Cedar Grove moved on from an affineur position, Wills asked if Brozak would be interested in tackling those duties. "I also went to seminars and talked to other affineurs. Some will share information; most will not."

Brozak is happy to share information; she staffs a hotline for those with questions about how to age cheese.

"A lot of the cheeses I handle have won some significant awards," Brozak says.

She also helps companies experiment with their cheeses. A recent sample involved a mild, four-month-aged sheep's milk cheese produced by Cedar Grove; Brozak treated the 10-pound cheese as a washed rind. Wills was upbeat about the cheese's prospects.

"I am enthusiastic about the new cheese. We will see whether it can be made that way consistently, but I took some of it home for my New Year's celebration," Wills said.

HIDDEN SPRINGS CREAMERY
AMY & TRAVIS FORGUES

Getting to Hidden Springs Creamery demands patience, a steady hand on the steering wheel, and a keen eye for unexpected vehicles. It is a rise and fall over steep, roller-coaster-type hills and requires maneuvering through curly two-lane roads about the width of a hiking trail, all while being careful to listen for the steady *clip-clop* of horse-drawn Amish buggies.

It is the essence of the Driftless Area, an unglaciated landscape with twists and turns and dramatic hills and valleys.

The reward lies at the top of a hill in rural Westby, in Vernon County, where Hidden Springs Creamery raises 700 sheep and produces noteworthy, award-winning cheeses. It is believed to be the only farmstead sheep cheese plant currently operating in Wisconsin.

Amy and Travis Forgues bought the creamery in April 2023, taking over from Brenda and Dean Jensen, who had founded and operated the farm and dairy for 15 years.

"It has been wonderfully overwhelming," says Amy, who became a licensed cheesemaker a few months after the purchase. In the interim, Brenda Jensen helped with the transition, sticking around for support and as the licensed cheesemaker.

The Hidden Springs domain includes three big barns for sheep of varying ages, a milking parlor, a cheese production and packaging area, and an underground aging cave, plus 74 acres with a view.

And the sheep themselves are quite a sight. Day-old lambs huddle together near a heat lamp, teetering on unsteady legs. Amy picks up one of the newborns and gives it tender cuddles while Travis bottle-feeds another. The older, milking sheep occupy themselves by munching on hay or grazing the pasture grass.

The sheep are the Lacaune breed—considered the Jersey of the sheep world—with genetics from France. "Their milk makes really rich, creamy cheese," Amy says. All of Hidden Springs' cheeses are made with milk that comes from their own sheep.

Hidden Springs' flagship cheese is appropriately called Driftless. It is a soft, creamy, spreadable sheep's milk cheese that's made in seven flavors. The natural flavor is "like chèvre but without the tang of a goat cheese," Amy says. Honey lavender won Best in Class in the 2023 U.S. Championship Cheese Contest, and cinnamon cranberry was named Best in Class in the 2022 World Championship Cheese Contest.

Milwaukee restaurateur and Chef Dan Jacobs, runner-up in Bravo TV's *Top Chef: Wisconsin* series in 2024, says Hidden Springs' Driftless is one of his favorite Wisconsin cheeses. "It's like a more basic but much better version of Boursin. It's really good on a grilled cheese sandwich; it adds a great layer of flavor," Jacobs says.

The newest Driftless flavor, released in 2024, is honey habanero. "Everyone wanted something a little spicier. Now it is one of our most popular flavors. It starts out sweet, and then ... whoo! You feel the heat," Amy says.

In December, Amy introduced a new product: ricotta made from the whey of the sheep's milk's curd—whey that would have been discarded otherwise.

Developing the ricotta was one of two steps that the Forgues took in late 2024 to reduce Hidden Springs' environmental impact. The other was installing solar panels to cut energy use.

FARMERS FROM VERMONT

Amy and Travis grew up in Vermont—another state known for its cheese—and both have farming backgrounds. Amy's family had a 220-acre maple sugar farm, dense with maple trees. Amy's grandfather collected sap with a team of horses pulling a wagon through the woods. Family and friends would ride behind on the wagon, jump off to pull the sap-filled buckets from the trees, and then pour the sap into a tank in the wagon. "This was a beautiful tradition of family and friends working together. It was a favorite childhood memory," Amy says.

Travis's family ran a dairy farm, raising cows, but they did not make cheese.

When Amy and Travis married, they moved to the Forgues family farm, had three children, and began their careers in agriculture. Travis ran the farm with his father, and they transitioned the

operation to organic and quickly became a leader within the organic industry. Amy tended to a three-acre blueberry farm, extensive gardens, and a small vineyard. She took cheesemaking classes at the University of Vermont and taught herself how to make cheese from cow's milk—for the family's personal use. She yearned to have a creamery to process the farm's milk into a value-added product, but the cost of building a facility from the ground up made it an impossible dream.

In the meantime, the dairy processing company that the Forgues farm in Vermont used was sold to a larger organization with a reputation for buying brands and dropping its farmers. Amy and Travis wanted more control over their destiny, so they contacted George Siemon, the founder of Organic Valley, a farmer-owned cooperative in La Farge, to see if they could become one of Organic Valley's farms. "He agreed to take our milk, but he said we would have to fill a truck with a load of milk to make the 2,100-mile drive from the Midwest financially feasible for Organic Valley. That meant banding together with other Vermont farmers, many of whom had to be coached through a transition to become organic. We signed on 60 farms, and together, our milk filled two trucks, every other day.

"We stabilized the income stream for those farms, and we were swept up in the mission of Organic Valley," Amy says.

Eventually, after 17 years at the Forgues farm in Vermont, Amy and Travis were offered jobs at Organic Valley. They moved to Wisconsin, and Travis served as executive vice president of membership and oversaw all farmer programs, while Amy ran a leadership development program for young farmer members.

That was until they heard that Hidden Springs was for sale and decided to take the leap.

Through Hidden Springs, Amy and Travis are still closely tied to relatives back in Vermont. Amy's sister sends maple syrup

from her farm for use in Hidden Springs' cheeses, and Travis's dad ships bales of hay for the sheep to eat. "It gives us a special connection and a further meaning to the food. Vermont maple syrup and Wisconsin cheese are the best of both states. And to use hay from Travis's family's farm to feed our animals is so gratifying.

"Travis's dad was here recently and wanted to see for himself how the sheep reacted to his hay. They like it! He watched the sheep eating his product, and it was very meaningful to him," Amy says.

THE SHEEP

The three barns separate the sheep by age and condition. One barn holds females about to give birth and their babies. At a visit to the farm last September, there were 180 lambing sheep and more than two dozen lambs less than one week old, *baaing* softly, in harmony. They were scrawny and walked on legs that were not yet sure of themselves, and when Amy picked them up, they snuggled in, like puppies.

The second barn houses lambs from two weeks to three months old, when they are ready to be sold or to graze on the pasture. Lambs are very susceptible to worms, so they don't go out to the pasture for the first 90 days, until their systems are more developed.

The third barn holds the milking flock, which averages 300 to 350 sheep at any point. "It could hold 1,000 sheep, but we're not going to pack them in like that," Travis says. On either side of a clean, concrete floor, the sheep spread out among stacks of hay, diligently chewing and seeking attention with their loud, low-pitched *baas*.

The milking sheep graze on the fenced pasture, heading out in orderly lines to the sloping fields. Two donkeys, Marilyn and her daughter, Peanut, keep an eye on and protect the sheep and lead them back to the barn when it's time. "Donkeys are protection animals, so if a predator like a bobcat or a coyote got into the pasture, the donkeys would scare them off with loud *braying* or would ultimately stomp them if they persist," Amy says.

At milking time, the sheep head into the small, tidy, vinyl-floored milking parlor, two dozen at a time. Each group is in the parlor for about 10 minutes, but when they are hooked onto machines, it takes only two minutes for the milk to be pumped out, Travis says. That means about 150 sheep can be milked in an hour.

Each sheep provides four pounds of milk a day, which is less than half a gallon. That compares to a dairy cow that can give 70 to 100 pounds a day, which translates into eight or nine gallons, or more.

"I think the Driftless Area is a perfect place to raise sheep because of the hills and the sandy soil," Amy says. "Sheep tread lightly, and that's good for erosion and soil protection."

SHEEP CHEESES

Amy is majority owner of Hidden Springs and head cheesemaker. She makes all of the cheese, with help from an assistant and now, also from Travis. In addition to heading farm operations, Travis earned his cheesemaker's license in November 2024.

Using sheep's milk to make cheese is not very different from using cow's or goat's milk, Amy says. "I prefer sheep's milk. The yield is much higher, the protein and fats are higher, and it's a creamier, richer milk." Amy credits Tony Hook, who buys Hidden Springs sheep's milk to use in Hook's cheese, as being "a really great mentor for me. And I have wonderful recipes from Brenda [Jensen]."

In addition to the Driftless spreadable cheeses, Hidden Springs makes Farmstead Feta, which is lighter and less salty than traditional feta cheese; Wischego, a Manchego-style cheese with a meaty flavor and notes of fermented fruit; Bad Axe, a mild, soft, rindless cheese that is aged for 30 days, and melts well for dishes like pizza; and Ocooch Mountain, a cave-aged, raw milk cheese with a washed rind that tastes nutty and buttery.

Hidden Springs' sheep's milk is also used in Bohemian Blue, a cheese produced by Hook's Cheese that is cave-aged, rindless, crumbly, and moist, with a taste that's both sweet and savory, reminiscent of salted caramel.

A new product recently joined the lineup. In fall 2024, Amy visited creameries in Italy to find out how they produce ricotta from whey. Whey is a natural byproduct of the cheesemaking process, and usually, it is considered a waste product that's spread on farm fields. But instead of discarding the whey, Hidden Springs has added a whey pump on its cheesemaking vat to turn it into Coulee Ricotta, which was introduced in December 2024.

Ricotta is called a cheese but it's actually a dairy product, like sour cream or yogurt, Amy says. It's made by heating the whey

high enough so the molecules "denature and link together to form delicate strands." Amy had to adapt the Italian recipe to work with her equipment. Also, she learned that Italian cheesemakers don't use cultures to make any of their cheeses.

"They depend on the local terroir to provide the bacteria. 'The culture is from the sheep's udder or on the cheesemaker's skin and clothes,' they would say. In the U.S., cheesemakers try to eliminate the natural bacteria," Amy says.

Hidden Springs' whey is also being upcycled in another way. Some of Amy's friends are opening Birch Point Distillery in Westby and using a portion of the whey to make vodka and gin.

Sustainability also comes into play at Hidden Springs through renewable energy. A solar array was installed in 2024 on the barn that houses newborn lambs and on the creamery. The solar panels are projected to generate 49.5 kilowatts of electricity, replacing 36 percent of the energy the farm and creamery are using and cutting electric bills substantially.

"This is about respecting the earth and the land. Our priorities— beyond making good cheese—are animal care and sustainability,"

says Amy. "We are making small strides to continue to make our farm more sustainable."

PLANNING FOR THE FUTURE

With less than two years of experience running Hidden Springs, Amy and Travis are adjusting to farming sheep, producing sheep's milk cheese, and all of the headaches and joys of running a business. "When we worked at Organic Valley, there were people who handled sales, people who handled marketing, people who worked with farmers, and people who worked in IT. Now, I'm doing all of those things," Amy says.

Several dairy innovation grants from the state of Wisconsin have helped Hidden Springs to become more efficient and grow, providing funds to obtain automatic filling equipment for the soft cheeses. "That was a game changer for us. We went from filling the cheese into tubs with spoons, by hand—which took about two full days to pack one batch of cheese—to the machine spitting out exact weight portions every three seconds. Now, we

pack the same size batch of cheese in four hours," Amy says.

She says other cheesemakers in Wisconsin have been very welcoming. "I do really feel supported. I think that is unique to this area."

Amish neighbors have also played an important role. Hidden Springs employs four Amish people, and they have been teaching Amy and Travis "the nuances of sheep farming as opposed to the cow farming that we were used to."

Hidden Springs also has a meat contingent to its business, working with Nordik Meats in Viroqua to make lamb sticks and sausages that are sold along with the company's cheeses.

Amy still has a small vegetable garden and blueberry patch at Hidden Springs, and bushes bursting with jewel-colored raspberries border the driveway.

The experience on the Forgues farm in Vermont "instilled in me and my children a respect for food and its origins. I learned how gratifying it is to be able to take something every step of the way."

As much as they are native Vermonters, Amy and Travis have come to love being in the Driftless region. "The Driftless is the only area in the Midwest that I would want to live," Amy says. "It feels very much like Vermont—the hills, the nature—it's just a beautiful area. Every time I come back, I am awed by the beauty."

Amy and Travis are trying to give back to some of their employees. Amy helped develop a sheep's milk soap business with Elmina, an Amish woman who helps birth the lambs, milk the sheep, and pack cheese. "When she gets married and moves next year, she will have something of her own and a connection to Hidden Springs," Amy says.

Meanwhile, Travis is helping Elmina's brother, Jonas, to learn cheesemaking so he can earn his own license.

"The goal is to create something bigger than yourself," Travis says.

Using sheep's milk for cheese is still relatively uncommon around the country. The U.S. is the biggest importer of sheep's milk cheese, and "we only make 1 percent of what we consume," Travis says, leaving a lot of room for growth in the industry.[1] He says it may be a matter of changing the public's perception; many people think sheep's milk will taste like goat's milk, but actually, it is creamier and doesn't have the distinctive goat's milk tang.

Travis tries to get that message across to shoppers at the Dane County Farmers' Market, waking even earlier than usual and driving about two and a half hours to set up a booth every week, offering samples of Hidden Springs cheeses.

"Our mission is to grow this. We hope to create jobs for life so small dairies can survive," he says.

1   John Umhoefer, "WCMA Notes: U.S. Sheep Cheeses Ever-Poised for Growth," Wisconsin Cheese Makers Association, January 5, 2024, https://www.wischeesemakersassn.org/news/wcma-notes-us-sheep-cheeses-ever-poised-for-growth-.

Name: Hidden Springs Creamery

Owners: Cheesemakers Amy and Travis Forgues

Community: Westby

Established: 2008

Website: hiddenspringscreamery.com

Retail shop: S1597 Hanson Road, Westby; by appointment only

Email: amy@hiddenspringscreamery.com

Tours: None

If Wisconsin were a country, it would be the fourth-largest cheesemaking country in the world, behind only the U.S., Germany, and France.

HOOK'S CHEESE
TONY HOOK

You could say that Tony Hook has helped put Mineral Point on the map.

Hook shook up the cheese world when Hook's Cheese first offered a 20-year-old cheddar in 2015—at the unheard-of price of $209 per pound—and it was all sold before the cheese was even ready to hit the market.

The dramatic release of the very-aged cheddar drew attention across the U.S., shining a light on both Hook's Cheese and its hometown: the historic community of Mineral Point, in Iowa County, about 45 minutes southwest of Madison.

But here in the Driftless, it may have been a little less of a surprise to see Hook step outside the box. A Wisconsin Master Cheesemaker who has been turning out award-winning artisan cheeses for more than 50 years, Hook smiles a lot when he talks about cheese. He takes great pleasure in playing around with cheese formulations and flavors, and tagging his creations with entertaining names.

Puns abound, such as Ewe'd Be Amazed, "a sweet, buttery, sheep's milk cheese with great melting potential," as the company describes it. There's Maaaahnterey Jack, a goat's milk version of Monterey Jack cheese, and Bang Bang Triple Play, a cow's, goat's, and sheep's milk mixture combined with three forms of peppers, resulting in a "heated explosion of flavors." One of Tony's favorites is EWE CALF to be KIDding, a blue cheese made from cow's, goat's, and sheep's milk with a sweet, nutty flavor. "It took two years before I came up with the cheese to match the name for that one," he says.

With seven employees—almost all family members—Hook's Cheese makes about 75 varieties of cheese, including six types of cheese curds, and uses cow's, sheep's, and goat's milk for its recipes. The cheeses have won all sorts of awards. Most recently, Little Boy Blue—a rich sheep's milk blue cheese with notes of grapes and honey that's aged for 10 to 12 months—won first prize in its class in the 2024 World Championship Cheese Contest. Tony took pride in that, "especially since we were going up against French Roqueforts."

And Tony never fails to proudly mention that it was his wife, Julie, also a cheesemaker, who scored a major coup when her colby cheese was awarded the top prize in the World Championship Cheese Contest in 1982, not only winning in her class but being named the best of all of the nearly 500 contenders from around the globe. She is still the only woman to achieve that distinction.

ART MERGES WITH HISTORY

Hook's Cheese resides in a 150-year-old limestone building that's on the National Register of Historic Places. It served as a livery stable for the guests' horses at the nearby Washington Hotel when it was built in 1875 in downtown Mineral Point, and became a cheese factory in 1929. At that point, it was one of five cheese factories in Mineral Point and about 3,200 throughout Wisconsin, Hook says. Today, the state has around 120 licensed dairy plants.

The weathered, beige stone exterior of the Hook's Cheese building may look simple and unobtrusive, but inside the building, Tony and his team are busy stirring up novel cheeses.

The cheesemaker and the city are a good fit; they are artistic companions. Mineral Point has long been known as a haven for artisans of all types, as it continues to be today, with several dozen painters, weavers, sculptors, writers, musicians, performers, and others. The nonprofit Shake Rag Alley Center for the Arts offers classes and workshops in a wide range of arts and crafts for adults and youths year-round, and about a dozen studios and art galleries populate the city of only about 2,600 residents.

One of the unique establishments on Mineral Point's High Street is the Republic of Letters bookstore, an independent bookstore owned by Keith Burrows and Leslie Damaso that opened in 2023, and The Book Kitchen, housed inside the Republic of Letters, that's owned by Nicole Bujewski and offers culinary classes year-round. Mineral Point is also the home of Little Creek Press, owned by Kristin Mitchell, an award-winning, independent publisher who focuses on publishing books by Wisconsin authors, telling stories about Wisconsin's history, places, and experiences.

It was not the art, but the lead ore that brought miners from Cornwall, England, to the Mineral Point area about 200 years ago, and they established a permanent settlement in 1827, making it Wisconsin's third-oldest city. So many historic homes and commercial structures are still standing and in use that much of the city is on the National Register of Historic Places, including about 500 buildings.

Tony Hook feels a connection to that sense of place. "Not only is our building historic, but being here for almost 40 years makes us part of the history of the whole community, too," he says.

MAKING CHEDDAR HISTORY

Tony's parents and grandparents were dairy farmers, but they didn't make cheese, and his parents sold their cows when Tony was five years old. He is the first in his family to become a cheesemaker. When he graduated from high school in 1970, he started working at the Barneveld Cheese Company, which was meant to be a summer job. But cheese was his fascination even after earning a bachelor's degree in business administration and

accounting from UW–Platteville. Hook earned his cheesemaker's license in 1972.

In 1976, Tony and Julie—who had met through high school friends and were married by then—were hired as cheesemakers at Buck Grove Cooperative, a farmer-owned co-op near Mineral Point that dates back to 1887. Tony managed the plant for several years, and at the same time, he and Julie started Hook's Cheese Company and sold their cheese under the Hook's name at Buck Grove. A decade later, it was time to go out on their own, and they bought the current 8,500-square-foot building in Mineral Point in 1987.

The new location prompted Hook to start experimenting with the concept of aging cheeses. It just so happened there was unused space available in the cold storage area.

"So, we decided to age some of the cheese. It was turning out well, so we kept doing it longer," Hook says. "At that time, nobody was aging anything beyond two or three years. As we aged it out longer, we felt we liked the cheese better and set more aside to age longer and longer."

They started with three years and moved on to five years, 10 years, and then 15. The first batch of the 15-year cheddar came out in 2009; there was about 500 pounds of it, selling at $50 a pound. "We started getting calls from all over; we didn't have enough to go around," Hook says. "Luckily, there was another batch ready a month later."

Eventually, they worked their way up to setting aside a batch of cheddar for 20 years.

It was a gamble … and the risk paid off. In that first small batch in 2015, all 450 pounds of the 20-year cheddar sold at a whopping $209 per pound. Since then, another two batches have come out, in 2020 and 2023. The next time Hook's will have some ready to go will be in April 2025.

The flavor and the texture of the cheddar change as it ages. Over the first five years, it becomes more acidic each year; after that, calcium lactate crystals begin to form. They start on the outside of the block and then follow suit inside the cheese. By 15 years, a sheet of crystals may be blanketing the exterior of a 40-pound block. The texture of the crystals is like a grainy salt, and the cheddar flavor is deeper and more mellow.

By 20 years, the cheese contains even more crystals that crunch when you bite them. "It has the texture of salt but it doesn't taste like salt," Tony says. Just put a shard of the cheese in your mouth and let it melt on your tongue to absorb all of the flavor. "It's very delicious, and a little exotic." If you want to indulge along with other food or a beverage, the 20-year cheddar pairs well with some red wines and fruits, like apples, or nuts, like almonds or pecans, he says, adding, "I like to just eat it by itself."

Will there be a 25-year cheddar? Tony is not quite ready to make a commitment—at least, not publicly. "Well, we might. In the 2025 batch, we may set aside some for a 25-year," he says, with a twinkle in his eye.

DRIFTLESS FLAVOR

Hook's Cheese is picky about where it gets milk; it comes from the same farms the company has been using for 46 years. "It all comes from within four miles of our cheese factory in downtown Mineral Point," Tony says. "The farmers all sign agreements that no hormones will be used, and they are all very small family farms, some going back for eight or nine generations. The biggest one has 45 cows. They are not huge conglomerate farms. When we need more, we get it from Lafayette Dairies, an Amish co-op."

The sheep's milk comes from Hidden Springs Creamery in Westby, and goat's milk is from LaClare Creamery near Fond du Lac.

"We make about 450,000 pounds of cheese a year," Hook says. "That's tiny compared to the big guys."

Being located in the Driftless Area is an important factor, Hook says. "I think the Driftless region is about the best area in this country to make cheese. As the glaciers came through, they dragged soil and vegetation through other areas of the country. But the glaciers didn't come through here. Our soil probably hasn't changed in a million years, and that really affects our grasses, flowers, and everything that grows in our area.

"Most of us—probably all of us in this area—believe that the Driftless produces a lot higher quality milk just because the water is filtered through the limestone. I also think our animal feed is a lot better because we get a lot better grasses in the rolling hills of southwest Wisconsin.

"We use high-quality milk, and we try to produce very high-quality cheese. The Driftless has a corner on the flavor, I believe. Of course, I'm a little prejudiced," Hook says.

THE OLD-SCHOOL WAY

The cheesemaking business has changed quite a bit since Hook started in the early 1970s, as far as milk availability, production goals, and clients. But one thing hasn't changed: the process by which cheese is made. It's still done the old-fashioned way at Hook's.

"We use open vats, and everything is done by hand, just like it was more than 100 years ago. We work over the vat. We cut the cheese by hand. We turn the slabs of cheese by hand every 15 minutes. We salt it by hand. We weigh it on a scale. Each vat can be produced a little bit differently to make the different cheeses," Hook says. "The big producers have big, closed tanks. Nobody even sees the cheese mixture. They have robots handling the blocks of cheese."

When Hook first started in the business, "we were competing with other area small cheese factories to get milk. Now, we all work together."

A few decades ago, Hook's was making large amounts of cheese and selling it to others for their use. "Very few were sold under our own label. We used to have a small area in back where we would sell our own cheese under our name."

That changed in 2001 when Hook began selling all of his cheeses under his own company's name. "We cut back on production. We used to make 1.5 million pounds of cheese a year, but it ended up on store shelves, mostly under someone else's label. We were just making commodity cheese. But to pay farmers for their milk, you need to bring in a little more money. We were already paying farmers more than most other companies, but under our own label at a higher price, we could pay them even more.

"We decided to make artisanal cheese, using smaller vats, that people would be willing to pay a premium for. We can't compete with the big guys who make one million pounds a day, so we have to have a niche," he says. "We were doing the work; we might as well let the customers know who's making it." Hook's cheeses are now sold in about 40 states and at the popular, weekly Dane County Farmers' Market in Madison.

Aging the cheese is one of Hook's Cheese's niches. Not only cheddar but Parmesan, Triple Play, and blue cheeses sit in the caves longer than most other cheesemakers, Hook says. "In the U.S., you have to age blue cheese for at least 60 days. We try to age most of our blues about a year or longer, except Blue Paradise, a double-cream blue, which sits for six months. We also age gouda and some of the goat's milk cheeses. Hurdy Gurdy, an Alpine-style goat cheese, sits for at least two years, and the flavor gets more intense."

Hook's has four cheese caves, one of which is 16 feet underground, and a cold storage area. The blue cheeses are kept separately from the other types, at a higher temperature and humidity "so we can get mold to grow. Once the blue is blue enough, it comes out of the cave and is sealed loosely in breathable bags and held in cold storage" at a colder temperature.

Hook's has done well with its blue cheeses in national and international competitions. The Little Boy Blue that was named top in its class at the World Championship Cheese Contest in 2024 has won awards "every year since we started making it in 2009," says Hook, who has earned the title of Wisconsin Master Cheesemaker in both blue and cheddar cheeses.

NATIONAL ATTENTION

Hook's Cheese got some special, national attention in 2024 when it was featured as an ingredient on the Bravo TV program *Top Chef: Wisconsin*—not once, but twice.

In the cheese-centric episode, Chef Danny Garcia used Hook's 15-year-aged cheddar in a savory churro. Chef Dan Jacobs used the five-year cheddar in a different episode during the series.

"It was pretty cool," Hook says. "It's great that all the chefs got to try everybody's cheese. They found out that Wisconsin cheese is excellent."

Residents of Mineral Point have known that for a while—at least, as far as Hook's Cheese is concerned. "They all know that fresh curd is ready on Fridays at 9 or 9:15 a.m. We can hardly keep up with the crowd until we close," says Tony.

Hook appreciates the local support he's gotten, and his philosophy is to return the favor. When the 20-year cheddars are released, Hook donates half of the proceeds to various causes. Past recipients have included the renovation of the UW–

Madison's Babcock Hall, which houses the Department of Food Science and the UW's dairy plant, and to Little John's Kitchen, a former Madison-area community kitchen that targeted food insecurity.

In 2023, several food pantries in southwest Wisconsin benefited from the special cheese. "We get from the community, and we've got to give back. That's the way it should be," Tony says.

Name: Hook's Cheese

Owners: Wisconsin Master Cheesemaker Tony Hook and cheesemaker Julie Hook

Community: Mineral Point

Established: 1976

Website: hookscheese.com

Retail shop: 320 Commerce Street, Mineral Point; open Monday through Friday, 8 a.m. to 2 p.m.

Phone: 608–987–3259

Tours: No tours, but the shop has a viewing window

Cheeses and cheesemakers in our book listed among *Bon Appétit's* 25 Most Important Cheeses in America: https://www.bonappetit.com/gallery/most-important-cheeses-in-america?srsltid=AfmBOoqB6WMZwxLkcps_LKXWVhZIly6t-8ev2cJ0XvqXQ8yGn6mcKzvl

LANDMARK CREAMERY
ANNA LANDMARK

Cheese was not Anna Landmark's first love.

The co-owner and cheesemaker at Landmark Creamery in Paoli, Anna Landmark's earlier career was high-pressure, ever-changing, and often frenetic.

Landmark was a political organizer, savvy and skilled. With a bachelor's degree in political science from the University of Wisconsin–Madison, Landmark managed campaigns, raised funds, recruited volunteers, and wrote advertisements for candidates and issues in Wisconsin and beyond.

"I've knocked on a lot of doors during my career," Landmark says.

Her father ran for the Wisconsin Assembly when Anna was in high school, and though he lost his race, that experience stirred Anna's interest in politics. While in college, she served as a page at the State Capitol and then volunteered for U.S. Senator Tammy Baldwin's first campaign for Congress. A Democrat/progressive, Landmark earned her political stripes in positions that included managing Dave Cieslewicz's successful campaign for Madison mayor in 2003 and serving as a state field organizer for then-U.S. Representative Dick Gephardt of Missouri. She also worked for One Wisconsin Now, a research and political advocacy hub for progressives.

But in 2008, after 14 years of a vagabond existence, crisscrossing the country to promote candidates in 12 states, Landmark was ready for a change. She was married and had a new baby daughter, Alice. "I got pretty burned out. It was very stressful, and I didn't want to move around anymore," she says.

She wanted to come home to the Mount Horeb area where she grew up, and had warm memories of her grandparents' dairy farm where she would feed the cows, play with the cats, and take the horses out on trail rides. "It was one of my favorite places. I spent a lot of time there," Anna says.

There were about 45 cows in the herd. "All the cows had names, and I would pet them while they were being milked. My grandfather always played polka music during the milking. He said it relaxed the cows, and they milked better."

And although her grandparents did not make cheese, it was a prominent feature at their farmhouse and a tribute to their Swiss heritage. "My grandparents always had a big block of Swiss cheese on the table. We would pick at it all day. Cheese was a constant; it was part of every meal."

So, Anna and her husband, Steve Elliott, bought five acres in the country in Albany, about 30 miles southeast of her childhood home. The family added a cow, a few sheep, goats, and horses. Landmark milked the cow and the goats and quickly accumulated an abundance of milk. She began playing around in the kitchen. "I like to make things from scratch," she says. "I learned how to make cheese and fell in love with it."

BREAKING INTO CHEESEMAKING

Sheep cheese was one of Landmark's favorites, and few cheesemakers were producing it at the time. It was an opportunity, and Landmark made it her goal. She took classes at the UW–Madison's Center for Dairy Research and won a scholarship from Wisconsin Cheese Originals (an organization that no longer exists). To earn her cheesemaker's license, she apprenticed at Cedar Grove Cheese in Plain for about a year, helping make vats of cheese, apply coatings, and wash cheese wheels. She also learned a lot about cheese caves, or aging rooms.

"Working in a cheese plant was really helpful. If you don't grow up in the cheese industry, even understanding the equipment is difficult and foreign."

Along the way, Landmark joined Soil Sisters, a nonprofit support and networking group for women farmers in southern Wisconsin. At one of the group's potluck dinners, Landmark met Anna Thomas Bates, then a *Milwaukee Journal Sentinel* recipe developer and food writer, whose former newspaper column, *Tallgrass Kitchen*, continued as a blog and evolved into other writing projects. Not only did the two Annas become fast friends, they decided to go into business together. Anna Landmark would make the cheese, and Anna Thomas Bates would promote and sell it.

Landmark Creamery began operating in 2014, buying milk from a local sheep farm, Enloe Brothers, in Rewey, which only milked

its sheep seasonally at the time. Anna Landmark developed and produced her company's cheese at Cedar Grove once a week, and Anna Thomas Bates sold it at the Westside Community Market in Madison. Regional distributors came on board, and Landmark cheese went out to cheese shops in Madison and around the country. Business slowly grew as the word spread.

By 2015, Landmark Creamery's Petit Nuage, French for small cloud—a soft, creamy sheep cheese (that's since been discontinued because it was so labor intensive)—began winning awards. In 2017, Landmark Creamery opened a retail shop in Paoli, in a small building that had housed a grocery store and then a pet food store. Offering made-to-order grilled cheese sandwiches featuring Landmark's artisan cheeses, the shop also displayed culinary specialty items from other food producers in Wisconsin and beyond. Behind the public store are four cheese caves where Landmark's cheeses age.

TROUBLES BREW

As Landmark Creamery was still establishing itself, two setbacks hit the young business hard.

Landmark had been aging some of its cheese in a cold storage facility in Monticello, about 15 miles away. Still struggling with startup costs, Landmark fell behind on its payments. In early 2019, even though Landmark had paid part of its debt, the owner of the storage building threw out pallet upon pallet of Landmark's cheese. More than 1,000 pounds of handcrafted cheese, valued at more than $20,000, wound up in a dumpster.

Several Madison chefs—members of the Culinary Ladies Collective, a nonprofit networking group of women who are professional chefs and growers—started a GoFundMe account and raised more than $14,000 for Landmark Creamery. But artisan cheese cannot be replenished quickly. Some types take six months or more to age, too long to meet the demand for many of Landmark's orders.

One year later, the second shoe fell: COVID-19. Foot traffic to the Paoli shop and farmers' markets slowed to a crawl. "Everything shut down super suddenly," Landmark says. It was a startling and scary time for small businesses.

Fortunately, Landmark Creamery had just moved its website onto a new platform with sophisticated online sales tools. "We realized we could set up an online shop almost instantly," Landmark says. She contacted farmers' market vendors who sold vegetables, meats, and other products and created a system for delivering all of their products together.

"We were sending out more than 200 orders a week for a year and a half," Landmark says. "That really helped us."

THE SEVEN ACRE CONNECTION

Today, Landmark Creamery produces 11 varieties of cheese—not counting all of the different flavors—made from sheep's or cow's milk. They include Anabasque, the company's signature Spanish Basque-style sheep cheese that's similar to gruyère; Brebis, a creamy, fresh sheep's milk cheese; Sweet Annie, a gouda-style sheep cheese; Rebel Miel, a soft, savory sheep's milk cheese washed in beer and mead; and fontina, a mild, melting cheese made from Brown Swiss cow's milk.

Landmark gets its sheep's milk now from a dairy in Juda, Ms. J and Co., which has enough sheep to provide milk year-round. So, while Anna still makes cheese once a week, she uses much bigger vats than before, producing about 150 wheels per batch.

Production moved in 2024 from Cedar Grove to a factory in Monroe, Wisconsin, owned by Chalet Cheese Cooperative, that used to make Swiss and Limburger cheeses. "It gives us a lot more capacity and room to grow," Landmark says.

After experiencing the healing power of collaboration during the pandemic, Landmark embarked on another joint venture in 2023, expanding the company's product line to butter in a partnership with Seven Acre Dairy, about one block from the cheesemaker's shop.

Seven Acre Dairy is a restored dairy factory in a building that dates back to 1888 and is on the National Register of Historic Places. It was a working dairy for nearly 100 years, making Swiss cheese and sweet cream butter. But the business closed in 1980, and the building went through several other incarnations. Then, in 2021, a group of local residents bought the building and renovated it, top to bottom, led by Nic Mink. Seven Acre Dairy now houses a restaurant and bar, a café, hotel rooms, and meeting spaces. Anna Landmark, who became a licensed butter maker in 2023, began churning there once a week while the public watches through viewing windows.

"They were looking for a dairy product to be produced inside the building, but they had little space for it. With butter, cream can be brought in cans, and the churn takes up only a small space," Landmark says.

The stainless-steel electric churn holds 50 gallons of cream at a time. Each batch needs two churns and yields about 400 pounds of butter. The butter business now includes cultured butter, with a bit of cheese culture; farmhouse butter, with a bit of whey; and compound butters, with a variety of flavors mixed in, from cinnamon maple to black garlic.

In late 2024, the collaboration between Landmark Creamery and Seven Acre Dairy expanded to become a full-fledged partnership, as Seven Acre bought out Anna Thomas Bates's half-ownership of Landmark Creamery.

"The partnership has slowly developed since Nic purchased the Seven Acre factory and began renovating it," Landmark says. The butter-making arrangement was the first step. "We've worked really well with each other."

Anna says the collaboration will help popularize the Landmark Creamery brand, opening marketing opportunities that her small cheese operation has not had. "I think Nic will bring his expertise to help us grow exponentially. It will let us ride on the Seven Acre coattails a little more and help us raise money that we need to expand."

Landmark Creamery will produce special cheeses for Seven Acre Dairy even as it continues to make its own cheeses, butters, and ice cream mixes, Anna says, and the two businesses will collaborate more on special dinner events.

Landmark also moved its retail shop and sandwich offerings to the lobby and counter service area in the Seven Acre building in early 2025, turning it into the Landmark Creamery and Café. Seven Acre continues to operate the restaurant and eight-room inn in the restored building at 6858 Paoli Road.

Landmark Creamery still runs its business out of its building at 6895 Paoli Road. The former shop area has been converted to host cheese tastings and private events, and racks of cheese wheels still fill the cheese caves.

CHEESEMAKING CHALLENGES

Anna Landmark is one of the few women cheesemakers in Wisconsin, but she says that has not been an obstacle for her. "The cheesemaking community in Wisconsin has been super welcoming. If I have questions, I can pick up the phone and get good advice."

The biggest challenge is that launching a cheesemaking business is very expensive. For one thing, it's hard to find the appropriate space to lease at existing plants. "We've only been able to make certain types of cheese because of equipment or space limitations," Landmark says.

It's also a very cash-intensive business upfront. "You spend a lot for milk. Sheep's milk costs about five times as much as cow's milk. And then you're sitting on cheese while it's aging for three months to 18 months. And food safety regulations have increased the cost. To build a cheese plant would cost a minimum of $1 million," Landmark says.

The high cost of sheep's milk makes Landmark cheeses more expensive, and as a result, it can be difficult to convince some cheese shops to carry them, says Anna.

Despite the challenges, Landmark has found her niche.

"What do I like about cheesemaking? All of it. I really enjoy the process. I love coming up with the recipes—there are a lot of fine details that you have to monitor. It's a great mix of science and craftsmanship, understanding how the curd feels but also what the pH meters are telling you [about the cheese's acidity]. With the stainless-steel tanks and heavy equipment, it's a somewhat industrial process, but the cheese is a living, breathing thing when you're done with it."

Anna's daughters, Alice, now a teenager, and Rose, 10, are part of the action and find it fun to work in the store, while son, Harrison, 12, has other interests.

NOTORIETY GROWS

Over the past 10 years, Landmark's cheeses have racked up more than 30 awards, including first prizes for Brebis, Arabesque, Pecora Nocciola, and Sweet Annie across the American Cheese Society competitions, U.S. and World Championship Cheese Contests.

Food & Wine magazine named Landmark Creamery one of the top 50 U.S. cheesemakers in 2021, saying, "Their washed-rind Anabasque is a wonderful example of cheesemaking's evolution in Wisconsin, where everything, and anything, appears to be possible."[1]

Anabasque is Anna's favorite cheese to cook with. It works well in fondues, casseroles, roasted potatoes, and even bitter

---

1   David Landsel, "The Best Cheese in America: These Are the Top 50 U.S. Cheese-makers," *Food & Wine*, December 27, 2021, https://www.foodandwine.com/lifestyle/best-cheese-america.

greens. She grates Pecora Nocciola, a pecorino-style sheep's milk cheese, on everything, especially pastas and salads.

New products are on the way, and Petit Nuage may come back if Landmark can invest in new equipment in a few years.

Being in the Driftless is a big part of Landmark Creamery's success ... and of Anna Landmark's joy.

"When I came back to Wisconsin, I knew that this was where I wanted to be. I love the area. I love the hills. Sheep are a really

good fit. They can use lands that are more marginal for grazing, and they are lighter on the land, using fewer resources," she says.

"Geography also matters quite a lot in cheese. I think the bedrock matters a lot. Even on farms where the animals are not grazing, the alfalfa grown locally comes through in the milk. There's a very specific flavor that gives you a sense that the cheese is from Wisconsin."

Name: Landmark Creamery

Owner: Cheesemaker Anna Landmark

Community: Paoli

Established: 2014

Website: landmarkcreamery.com

Retail shop: Landmark Creamery and Café,
inside Seven Acre Dairy, 6858 Paoli Road, Paoli

Phone: 608-848-1162

Tours: Cave tours and cheese tastings;
tickets are available on the website

Cheesemakers in our book who sell their cheese
at the Dane County Farmers' Market:

Brunkow Cheese, Schroeder Käse, Hook's Cheese,
Hidden Springs, Bleu Mont Dairy, Capri Cheese

Capri Cheese also has a booth at the
Northside Farmers' Market.

Landmark Creamery has a booth at the
Madison Westside Community Market.

Sarah Bekkum can stand on the spacious wooden porch outside Nordic Creamery in rural Westby and look across the sloping meadows at the farmstead where she grew up. The land has been in her family for four generations since her great-grandparents, Ole and Lena Langaard, immigrated from Norway in 1917 and began dairy farming on the property.

Sarah's husband, Al Bekkum, was born and raised just a few miles away, also in Vernon County.

In this hilly, rustic, pastoral setting in the Driftless, Al and Sarah run a bustling cheese and butter business that sends their products around the country, including to some of the Midwest's finest restaurants and hotels.

The Bekkums launched Nordic Creamery in 2007. They built their cheesemaking plant right on their western Wisconsin farm in 2011, after racking up thousands of miles and hundreds of hours driving to Cedar Grove Cheese in Plain or Pasture Pride Cheese in Cashton, where Al would make his cheeses, and to Sassy Cow Creamery near Columbus, to produce butters.

Sarah and Al and about a dozen employees make more than 40 varieties of cheeses and butters from the milk of cows, sheep, and goats. They are known for their artisanal butters. Another of their specialties is cheese using A2 milk. This protein differentiation seems to make milk products more palatable for some consumers.

Owning and operating a creamery was not a burning career goal for either Al or Sarah in their early years. Sarah was a medical lab technician. Al took a job in construction after he graduated from high school. But when wintry weather set in, he was laid off and needed work. A local dairy, Westby Cooperative Creamery, was looking for help, and Al got the job.

It was at the Westby plant that Al and Sarah met. Al had become a cheesemaker, and Sarah worked in the lab, testing milk for bacteria and quality control. Today, they have six children, three of whom work with them at Nordic Creamery, as well as seven dogs and a host of animals that have no connection with the dairy business.

But the Bekkums are not what you might imagine to be a typical cheesemaking family. While they are passionate about their cheeses and butters, they have some side businesses, too. For one thing, they also raise beef cattle and pigs, and sell the meat at their shops along with their dairy products.

And there's more. They raise horses for harness racing and Amish buggies. And they foster thousands of baby chicks for nearby egg producers. They also grow corn and hay to feed their menagerie, which includes contingents of cows, goats, and sheep—just for fun.

With all of their endeavors, the Bekkums work seven days a week. "We love to be busy," says Sarah. No doubt, a major understatement.

Last summer, Al and Sarah scored a first: they took a real vacation, a seven-day cruise to Alaska. "It's the longest we've ever been away from the farm," Al says. "It was very enjoyable."

SPECIALTY CHEESES

When the Bekkums opened Nordic Creamery, it was a homestead dairy. They acquired their own small herd of about 35 dairy cows. Sarah and one of the couple's sons would get up early in the morning and milk the cows, and Al used the milk to make cheese and butter. "That's how we wanted to be—the hands-on little guy. You know all of your cows' names and are really passionate about the lifestyle," Sarah says.

But after several years, they realized it was a lot of work to manage a herd, milk cows, make cheese and butter, and raise six children.

Now, Nordic Creamery gets its milk primarily from Amish farmers who live within 15 miles of the creamery and milk their cows, goats, and sheep by hand.

Nordic produces a wide variety of cheeses using cow's milk, including 10 types of cheddar, mozzarella, Parmesan, Muenster, and cheddar curds. There are several types of cheese using sheep's or goat's milk, and some mixed milk cheeses.

Grumpy Goat aged goat cheddar is the biggest seller among their goat cheeses, Al says. "It's a unique taste and a unique label. I get comments about it all the time." Compared to an aged cheddar made from cow's milk, it is "very smooth, with a little bit of a bite from the aging. There's a great nutty flavor to it and a sharpness like aged cow cheddar.

"We pride ourselves on using fresh goat's milk; there is no strong goat taste in our cheeses," he says.

Another popular product is Capriko, a semi-hard cheese made from goat's and cow's milk. "It was the first mixed milk cheese that I ever made. It came out in first place at the American Cheese Championships in Chicago in 2008 and won the 2009 World Cheese Championship gold medal in its class," Al says. "The contest was held in the Canary Islands. I didn't get to go—I couldn't be away from the farm."

Here's how the idea for Capriko came about: When the business started, Nordic was often working with goat cheese, and it could be a hard sell for consumers, Al says. "I was doing demonstrations in stores. Customers would ask about the samples, and as soon as they heard it was goat cheese, they would walk past and not taste it. So, I thought I'd like to try something different that would not be as pungent. I decided to blend cow's and goat's milk together in a cheddar. You can taste the goat right away, and it finishes with a subtle cow's milk taste."

A2 CHEESES

More recently, Nordic Creamery specializes in A2 milk cheese products. A2 refers to a type of milk lacking a protein called A1, and it seems to be easier for people to digest. It has been researched for 20 years by scientists in New Zealand.

A couple of customers had asked for A2 milk products, so Al decided to look into it. It comes from cows with a particular genetic structure, and Guernsey and Jersey cows are more likely to have it, he says. Two Amish dairy farmers in the area tested their animals and found that many had the right genes to produce A2 milk. "We asked them to get rid of the cows without the A2 gene and buy more of those with it. Now, we only use milk from those two farms for our A2 cheese," he says.

A2 milk is just 0.5 percent of total milk sales in the U.S. retail market, according to Circana data for the 52 weeks ending Oct. 6, 2024, says Suzanne Isige, director of market research for the Dairy Farmers of Wisconsin.[1] Figures for wholesale use and cheese production were not available.

Nordic makes about 20 cheeses with the A2 protein, including regular, smoked, and flavored cheddars and mozzarella. "Sales are good, but a lot of people are still just learning about the product," Sarah says. "For some, though, the A2 has been life-changing for their family."

BETTER BUTTER

Nordic began making butter in 2011. At the time, Nordic was believed to be the first homestead creamery in Wisconsin to make butter commercially from its own cows. It began as a side gig after customers at Chicago's Green City Market—where the Bekkums were selling Nordic cheese—asked if they had butter, too. Today, dozens of upscale restaurants and hotels in the Chicago area, the Twin Cities, throughout Wisconsin, and around the Midwest are Nordic Creamery's butter customers.

And with good reason. Three of their butter flavors took home awards from the 2024 World Championship Cheese Contest: Pepper Butter, first place; Honey Butter, second place; Garlic Butter, third place. In 2023, their Cinnamon Sugar Butter won first prize at the World Dairy Expo and second prize at the World Championship Cheese Contest.

"Butter was a second thought for us," says Sarah. "Now, butter makes up a smidge over half of our business."

Artisan butter is a relatively new product in Wisconsin, Al says. "When we started making it, there wasn't anybody else

---

1   Milk Monthly Retail Snapshot, Circana (Data through 10-06-2024).pdf.

doing it. We were at the forefront. We got help from the state's Department of Agriculture and other agencies. They were excited that somebody wanted to do it. There wasn't even a category for flavored butters in any cheesemaker competitions. As of a few years ago, there were only about 35 licensed butter makers in Wisconsin," Al says. He is one of them.

Most of Nordic's butters are made with regular cow's milk, but one type is made with goat's milk. Goat's and sheep's milk butters are "a lot smoother, softer butter with a lot lower melting point. They're a very nice product. We use cow and goat butter in pastries at home for the family, especially Norwegian pastries for the holidays, like krumkake," Al says.

Artisan butter is very fresh and should be used as soon as possible. Al says customers in Chicago snapped up the butter when he introduced it. "We would make it on Fridays and take it to the Green City Market in Chicago's Lincoln Park on Saturdays, and people would line up to buy it as far as you could see."

PANDEMIC PANIC

When the COVID-19 pandemic hit in spring 2020, it was a scary time for Nordic Creamery, but ultimately, it launched a big increase in sales.

Nordic had a retail shop at the plant, but the Bekkums had purchased some property in Westby and were planning to renovate it and move the shop there. Before that could be accomplished, the pandemic hit. The store at the plant closed, and many restaurants across the country either closed temporarily or severely limited their hours, affecting Nordic's wholesale orders. "One distributor had an order in, but their buyer—whom I've known for years—had to cancel. Another distributor wouldn't even put in an order," Al says.

"I was getting nervous, wondering, *Would I have to lay off*

employees? We went out and talked to our farmers and said we may have to cut milk orders because I'm not sure that we can move the product."

So, the Bekkums decided to focus on online orders, shipping products directly to customers' doors. Taking a cue from Amazon, the Bekkums enlisted a local delivery service and offered a special sale on Nordic's website to people living in the Upper Midwest within the company's delivery area.

"Online was never a big thing for us, other than gift boxes at the holidays. But we tried to fix the situation to stay afloat. We went from the normal one to two orders a week at that time of year, worth about $50 to $100 on a good day, to more than $1,000 a day in online sales. We turned our store at the plant into a shipping center, and it's been that way ever since," Al says. While the momentum has tapered since then, the move was a revelation that helped the Bekkums realize the power of online shopping.

About two months after the nationwide pandemic shutdown, distributors were putting in orders at double and triple the previous size, and people who were still spending much of their time at home "didn't just want commodity products. March and April of 2020 looked pretty bad, but the year turned out to be our best year, up to that point," Al says.

The new retail shop in Westby opened in the spring of 2021 and remains open. Nordic also has a pop-up shop in a mall in La Crosse during the holiday season.

ANIMAL FARM

The horses came later—at least, as a business.

Al and Sarah used to have a few horses at the farm for the family to ride. But they didn't think about horses as a business until about 10 years ago, when one of their employees, a neighboring Amish man, needed draft horses. Al said he would go to a horse auction and look for a team that could help with the neighbor's field work and might also be used for hay rides. "We bought the team … and I got the bug to buy more horses," he says.

And he branched out. A friend was a harness racing fan and suggested Al try training a horse he had purchased. "He had such a good pedigree. That first year, he raced at a track near the Twin Cities; each time, the horse would finish last, and then we had a three-hour drive home." At the end of the racing season, all of the horses that had competed were allowed to race for a final time. "They paraded the horses before the start, and he came out of the barn, acting goofy. We watched the race … and he came from behind and won." The Bekkums took home a $17,500 purse. "We were on a high and got hooked pretty bad," Al says.

Today, they own 85 horses and keep most of them on the farm. About 30 are used to work in the fields or in pulling competitions, and the others are harness racers.

The Bekkums also raise chicks—about 50,000 of them. From the time the birds are one day old until they are 16 weeks old, they are housed in a huge barn on the property where the Bekkums give them organic feed, provide water, and look after them every day. Then they are hauled off to other farms where their mission is to lay eggs.

While cleanup may sound like a drag, there are benefits to it. "Chicken poop helps us grow some amazing crops," Al says.

A handful of beef cattle and pigs are also raised on the farm—some for the family's use and some to sell in the Westby store. "They graze like everything else around here," Sarah says. In addition to the standard animal feed, the Bekkums' cows and pigs get to eat some of the whey that's a byproduct of the cheese production. "They do enjoy a hot tote of whey, especially in the winter," she says.

Fourteen goats are also part of the menagerie. Al and Sarah bring some of their animals to the shop in Westby, where they have a barn and a small petting zoo with goats, sheep, horses, and calves. "They stay there for the summer. We rotate them," Sarah says.

For Al and Sarah, life is busy, but they have been able to choose the ways they want to be busy.

"I like doing something that not a lot of other people are doing," Al says. "What makes us unique as human beings is that we have these differences. To make a product that's a little different and then to get the recognition that people enjoy that product, that's what makes us happy."

Name: Nordic Creamery

Owners: Cheesemakers Al and Sarah Bekkum

Community: Westby

Established: 2007

Website: nordiccreamery.com

Retail shop: 202 West Old Towne Road, Westby;
open Monday through Saturday 10 a.m. to 5 p.m.,
and Sundays 11 a.m. to 3 p.m. May through September

Phone: Store 608–634-FARM (3276); plant 608–634–3199

Tours: Not currently available

Wisconsin has about 1,200 licensed cheesemakers;
107 have earned a Master Cheesemaker designation
since that program began 30 years ago.

WALTER ROELLI
SHULLSBURG, WIS.

ROELLI CHEESE HAUS
CHRIS ROELLI

You can feel the sense of history even before you walk in the door at Roelli Cheese Haus near Shullsburg, just a few miles north of the Illinois border in Lafayette County.

The wooden sign near the shop door, "Cheese of all kinds for sale," dates back to the 1930s.

Parked in front is a dark green 1945 Chevy pickup truck with wooden panels along the cargo bed and Walter Roelli's name on the side door. It's the same model that Walter drove around in those days to haul milk. Amazingly, a 1945 Chevy pickup was found in Nebraska and repainted to look like the original.

In the 1940s and early '50s, Walter would stand 25 cans in the back of the truck every day and drive to as many as 10 nearby farms, filling each can with about 100 pounds of milk and bringing the haul to the factory to transform it into cheese.

These days, it is Walter Roelli's grandson, Chris Roelli (pronounced RAH-lee, as in JOLLY) who is in charge of cheesemaking duties. Chris is the fourth generation of his family in the cheese business.

"It's a kind of lifestyle. I didn't know any different," he says.

It's more than just a tradition. Chris Roelli is a Wisconsin Master Cheesemaker, and his cheeses have drawn high marks in industry competitions. Roelli's sweet spot is cheddar blue, a combination of the two popular cheeses into the company's Dunbarton Blue and Red Rock cheeses. "Dunbarton was our lightning in a bottle; it allowed us to build a national sales network. Red Rock was the answer to what buyers would ask: What else do you have? Now, Red Rock is our No. 1 selling cheese," Roelli says. "They really put our brand on the map and allowed us to grow."

Roelli's Red Rock was named one of the top 20 cheeses in the 2022 World Championship Cheese Contest, and Dunbarton Blue ranked third in its class in the 2024 World Championships.

Dunbarton is modeled after a traditional English farmhouse cheddar, Roelli says. "It is full-flavored, somewhat salty, and savory, with a drier texture and slightly earthy note. We add in just a hint of a blue vein to give it a slight hint of a blue cheese flavor."

Dunbarton is "the jazz of blue cheese," according to a 2018 article in *Bon Appétit* magazine that lists it among the "25 most important cheeses in America."[1]

---

1   Carey Polis, "25 Most Important Cheeses of America, According to Cheese Experts," *Bon Appétit*, April 25, 2018, https://www.bonappetit.com/gallery/most-important-chees-es-in-america?srsltid=AfmBOoodIn_5IUa5ig_joqXf7YVzAuJwdTpDlzZoDLQMX9_NBIHFaM5R.

Red Rock is an American sister to the English-style Dunbarton. "It's made the way we make cheddar in America, mild and mellow with a fudgy texture, annatto for color, just enough savory flavor to wake it up, and a nice earth note from the natural rind. There's just a hint of blue flavor to really set it apart," Roelli says.

Visually, Dunbarton is a pale, creamy color, and Red Rock is a striking orange. The blue in both cheeses looks like a gash—a straight line or two that's almost like abstract art.

Dunbarton Blue was one of the cheeses featured on Season 21 of Bravo's *Top Chef* series, which was based in Wisconsin. Chef Rasika Venkatesa used the Dunbarton with chicken thighs and rice cakes to make an Indian dish called paniyaram that drew warm praise from the judges.

"It was fun to watch, fun to have that national audience," Roelli says. He was one of half a dozen Wisconsin cheesemakers who were invited to meet with the producers around two years ago to help pitch the concept of a dairy-centric theme for *Top Chef*, explaining how significant the dairy industry is to Wisconsin. When the show eventually was filmed in summer 2023, "everything was top secret," Roelli says. "We filmed all day, and only about 15 minutes of it aired in the episode in 2024. It was a unique experience."

Milwaukee Chef Dan Jacobs, runner-up in the *Top Chef: Wisconsin* series, features Red Rock on the menu of his restaurant EsterEv. "It's one of the most interesting cheeses that comes out of Wisconsin," Jacobs says.

EsterEv uses the cheese as part of a play on a cheeseburger donut. The Red Rock is turned into a meltable cheese that fills a donut made with beef fat, adorned with a special sauce of pickled ramps and mustard, as a faux Thousand Island dressing.

INSIDE ROELLI CHEESE HAUS

That brush with Hollywood—or, in this case, the Milwaukee area, since the main challenge of the *Top Chef* cheese episode was filmed there—was a contrast to the down-home flavor of the Roelli Cheese Haus store and cheesemaking plant.

Inside the shop, dozens of miniature, scale-model trucks line high shelves that run across most of the store's perimeter. Chris's father collected them. Many of the trucks reflect the dairy industry, like Dean Foods and Associated Milk Producers Inc., while others are just fun, like Toys "R" Us.

"They've been there for most of my life. Dad displayed them for so many years. They're kind of a conversation piece," Chris says. His dad, Dave Roelli, is no longer involved in the day-to-day operations, but he is in the shop often. "His thumbprint is all over this place, as well as my grandfather's and my uncles'."

The shop is a snacker's delight, with candy, popcorn, jams, mustards, soda pop, and beer, many of them made in Wisconsin, and prepared deli sandwiches enhanced with Roelli cheese.

Cheese is clearly the star, featuring dozens of varieties made by Roelli and other Wisconsin cheesemakers, filling the refrigerated display cases and available for purchase. A row of red, white,

and blue ribbons sits prominently over the cases, showing off the many awards that Roelli cheeses have won over the years.

WHERE THE ACTION IS

Across the driveway from the store is the plant where Roelli cheeses are made, and attached to the factory is the small home where Chris and his wife, Kristine, live. All four generations of Roelli cheesemakers have lived there at some point. Work and life, intrinsically and intricately connected.

"As a kid, we lived off the premises in Darlington, seven miles north. But I was always here with my dad," Roelli says. "My earliest memories of working with my dad in the plant: when I was in middle school, I'd be sweeping the floors and taking trash out, jobs to keep me busy. Cheesemaking got into my blood."

Inside the factory door, a poster heralds "Grand Champion Cheesemaker Chris Roelli." It was presented by the Foreign Type Cheesemakers Association in 2018 during the Cheese Days festival in Monroe.

In the cheese production room, employees wearing blue shirts with the lettering "curd crew" are making Roelli's Red Rock cheese. Four-pronged stirring knives push through a stainless-steel vat filled with about 10,000 pounds of the milk mixture, which contains mold cultures for both cheddar and blue cheeses. Roelli moves the curds forward with his hands, and employees help rake the curds to the front, "trenching" the cheese. The liquid whey is drained out, and the curds are compressed into loaves that will be turned every 10 to 15 minutes until the whey develops the right acidity, which takes about an hour and a half for Red Rock. It's a process called cheddaring. The cheese will be pierced to let air in and allow the blue cheese mold to bloom, and then the cheese is aged, from 60 days to one year.

"Certain cultures are designed to die, and other cultures feed on them. The mold mellows the cheese, creating a pathway from the outside air to the center of the block," Roelli says. "The cheese will taste different from day one to day sixty."

The whey, which is collected in an adjacent silo, will be spread on the fields of nearby farmers.

A 100-YEAR FAMILY TRADITION

Chris Roelli's Wisconsin cheesemaking story begins with his great-grandfather, Adolph Roelli, who grew up in Switzerland and came to the U.S. in 1906. Adolph was the youngest of 13 children in his family. He had learned cheesemaking in Switzerland and then interned with his uncle in France, where the cheesemaking system was very regimented. He came to the U.S. looking for a better life and lived in Ohio at first, with a group of Swiss immigrants. Then, Adolph was hired by the Hicks Cheese Co-op in Wisconsin and moved here. "The same facility that I'm living and working in," Chris says.

The family's trove of documents includes Adolph's cheesemaker's license, earned in 1924. It was his job to make whatever types of cheese the co-op members requested. Receipts dating back to those days show the products included cheddar, Limburger, brick, colby, Emmental, and Muenster. For 50 pounds of cheese, customers paid $7.67. "I would get that for a quarter-pound of Red Rock right now," Roelli says.

Adolph owned a farm a few miles from the plant, "very near where I pick up my milk now," Chris says, but Adolph's wife died young, leaving him with four children to raise. He decided it would be easier to take care of the family in the little house at the cheese factory.

Living at the factory was common practice for cheesemakers in the early 1900s, Chris says, simply because of the logistics of the work. There was no mechanical way to keep milk cool,

no refrigeration or electricity in rural Wisconsin until the late 1930s. When they milked their cows, they had to make cheese right away because there was no way to keep the milk fresh. A lot of them made cheese in the morning, noon, and night, Chris says.

Adolph's son, Walter—Chris's grandfather—eventually took over and later bought the Hicks Cheese Co-op. He changed the name to Roelli Cheese.

By the time Chris's father, Dave, managed operations as the third generation of cheesemakers in the family, Roelli Cheese Haus was a large-volume plant that cranked out 35,000 to 40,000 pounds of cheddar cheese each week, to be sold under the brand names of its clients.

And then, in 1991, the unforeseen happened. The market for cheddar cheese collapsed. Too much milk was being produced. So much that dairy farmers were pouring their milk down the drain, and the federal government was buying millions of pounds of cheese, storing it in warehouses, and giving it away to needy families—a practice that continues today, Roelli says.

"Farmers are not unique. Like every other business, they want to grow. At that time, growing often meant buying more cows. Just as it is today for dairy farms, you were either getting bigger or you were getting run over," Roelli says. More cows meant more milk, but there weren't enough buyers to purchase the excess.

The oversupply happened again during the COVID-19 pandemic. A big part of the dairy industry revolves around food service. During the pandemic, people couldn't go out to restaurants to eat, so chefs were not using up as much cheese as usual, and children were kept home from school, so they didn't get their cartons of milk.

"Milk is produced every day, and so is cheese. If there is a major downturn and the cheese doesn't move, when you fill the storage space, you have major problems. You end up dumping milk. The supply chain is very tight; it doesn't take much of a hiccup to upset that," Roelli says.

At the point of the 1991 downturn, Roelli Cheese already had been operating on a slim profit margin of two cents per pound of cheese sold, and the plant's equipment was old and worn and would soon need to be updated. "Most of it was installed in the 1950s, so it was pretty well used up. Replacement costs were in the millions. My dad was burned out. His passion fizzled."

Not wanting to strap Chris with huge debt, Dave closed the cheese plant. But the family never veered far from cheesemaking. Father and son drove a milk-hauling truck and then ran a trucking company. "I wasn't so good at that. I learned a lot of business lessons," Chris says.

GOING ARTISAN

By 2006, artisan cheese was gaining attention, and Chris felt the pull to get back into cheesemaking, but on a smaller scale. He opened Roelli Cheese Haus at the same property that had stayed in the family all these years, and he co-owns the business with his first cousin, Jason Roelli.

The company includes milk hauling and cheese trucking. Chris is in charge of cheese production and aging. A new cheese cellar was built in 2012, big enough to hold 250,000 pounds of cheese.

Roelli Cheese Haus makes 15 types of cheese, totaling about 200,000 pounds of cheese a year, and while that may sound like a lot, it is within the smallest 5 percent of cheesemakers in the U.S., Chris says, and is about one-tenth of the amount his father and grandfather produced.

Roelli buys milk from a local co-op and uses the same farmer's milk every day. The farm is within five miles of the cheese plant. "Animal husbandry is really big on my radar. I see the cows and how they are treated; I feel comfortable that these cows produce the best milk. And using the same cows' milk, you become intimately familiar with how the milk reacts to the enzymes that we use," he says.

"The issue is control. I am able to control the quality far more than if I were buying commingled milk. I consider this our niche, our ace in the hole."

Being located in the Driftless Area helps make the cheese unique, too. "At the end of the day, it comes down to water filtration. The limestone deposits in the region are an important part of the water filtration that goes into our aquifers. The cows drink a lot of water. It's in the greens on the pasture or the hay in the winter—they still have the moisture that comes out of the earth. It has an amazing effect on the taste and flavor of the milk. It's one of the reasons a lot of immigrants from Europe ended up here. They found out early on that we are in an area that produces products that are on par with or even better than what they had back home," Roelli says.

To say that Roelli loves being a cheesemaker is putting it mildly. "I'm comfortable in the cheese factory. It's an artistry lifestyle. You get to see the fruits of your labor every day. And sometimes it's six months or a year from the day you made it."

Since Chris began Roelli Cheese Haus, the whole family has helped in some capacity over the years. Chris is in charge of the factory, while Kristine manages the retail shop, and their two children pitch in where they're needed.

"The goal is to have the cheese be better every time. It's just really neat to see what happens when everything is working right: the farmer, the cows, the feed, our sanitation program. Milk is a living organism, and no two days are the same. It's the same manufacturing procedures, but the cheese is always in control. My job is to steer it in the right direction," says Chris.

Will there be a fifth generation of the Roelli family making cheese? "We don't know yet," Chris says. "It's a hard business, especially on the artisan side. It's a seven-days-a-week, 365-days-a-year job. You have to have the passion, to really enjoy it, to make it work. Very few people get rich doing it."

Regardless of how that turns out, he adds, "I'm really proud of what we've built."

....

Name: Roelli Cheese Haus

Owner: Wisconsin Master Cheesemaker Chris Roelli

Community: Shullsburg

Established: 2006

Website: roellicheese.com

Retail shop: 15982 State Highway 11, Shullsburg; open Monday through Friday 8 a.m. to 5 p.m., Saturday 8 a.m. to 4 p.m., Sunday 10 a.m. to 4 p.m. Hours may vary by season.

Phone: 608–965–3779

Tours: None

....

Today, there are about 120 licensed cheese plants in the state.

SCHROEDER KÄSE

BRYON SCHROEDER

It isn't very common to find a cheesemaking plant smack-dab in the middle of town, just off Main Street, but that's where you'll find Schroeder Käse (pronounced SHRAY-der CASE) in historic Darlington, producing a French-style brie so well respected that it appeared on Bravo TV's *Top Chef: Wisconsin* in 2024.

Nestled along the Pecatonica River in Lafayette County, Darlington is a community of 2,500 whose Main Street is populated by so many century-old buildings that the entire six-block stretch is on the National Register of Historic Places.

It's a place where you can buy a fresh, house-made donut at a local café and spend less than $10 for a hearty hamburger for lunch, and where motorists stop politely for pedestrians waiting at a crosswalk.

At the entrance to Darlington's downtown, a 56-foot-tall monument, topped by the statue of a Union soldier, greets visitors. Sculpted from Vermont granite, the monolith honors the memory of all the soldiers and sailors who fought in the Civil War.

Along Main Street, long-standing buildings proudly display the year they were built, like the red brick pharmacy building dating back to 1880, and two doors down, the 1896 building that currently houses a clothing store. The 1883 Driver Opera House was getting a facelift as workers on scaffolds touched up the trim, on a crisp autumn day.

Bird sculptures stand guard outside businesses and in public places. There's the great blue heron perched in front of the "Welcome to Darlington, The Pearl of the Pecatonica" sign along the Pecatonica River and the bluebird stationed within a bed of flowers near the Schroeder Käse plant. Created from fiberglass by sculptor Dave Oswald of Sparta and painted by Darlington residents, the statues help illustrate Darlington's status as a member of Bird City Wisconsin, part of a network of bird conservation programs.

Fronting on Ann Street—all of the side roads off Main Street are named for women—is the relatively modern building that houses Schroeder Käse. But what you'll notice first is the huge mouth of a shark, its gaping jaws wide open and teeth bared, mounted on a trailer along with a sign that teases, "Say Cheese!" If the shark mouth looks familiar, there's a good reason. It is a memento from a premiere of one of the *Jaws* movies and was purchased by a former owner of the property.

Behind that menacing mouth, in a building that used to serve as a gas station, cheesemaker Bryon Schroeder crafts cheddar cheese curds, triple-crème brie cheese, and double-crème and triple-crème gorgonzola blue. A licensed cheesemaker, Schroeder represents the third generation of his family to work in the cheese industry, and he is teaching his son, Cameron, to become the fourth.

"My grandpa owned a cheese factory. When I was little, I rode on the milk truck with Dad after school and on weekends. When I turned 13, I started helping Grandpa and my uncles make cheese," Schroeder says. After he graduated from high school, he worked at the cheese plant full-time and earned his cheesemaker's license at age 22.

"I did everything at Grandpa's cheese factory. I made the cheese and packaged it, handled pasteurization and sanitation, too,"

Schroeder says. "We made a lot of marble jack, combinations of cheddars and colbys with Monterey Jack, and blue cheeses, too."

In 2005, a large Wisconsin cheese manufacturer bought the factory. Schroeder was plant manager for that company until 2012, when he went to work for another cheese manufacturer. In 2016, he decided it was time to start his own business. Schroeder Käse was established, and Bryon was the sole employee until Cameron joined him as an apprentice, a few years ago.

LONG DAYS

Making cheese is not a nine-to-five job; it takes a lot of hours and a lot of patience.

Here's how an average day starts for Bryon: He wakes up at 2:30 or 3 a.m. and makes the 35-minute trip from his home in Rewey to the Darlington cheese plant. After sanitizing the milk truck, he has a 30-minute drive to the farm near Platteville that supplies Schroeder Käse with milk. There, he tests the milk temperature, loads 4,200 pounds of milk in the truck, and hauls it to Darlington. Back at the plant, Bryon checks for antibiotics and pasteurizes the milk.

Then, it's time to start making cheese or yogurt.

Pasteurizing one batch of milk takes four hours; then, it is pumped into a vat and transformed into cheese, which takes another two to four hours. The brie and blue cheeses are poured into molds, where they will age, while the cheddar curds must be matted, milled, and packaged for immediate sale.

When Schroeder Käse opened, Bryon produced hand-stretched string cheese and fresh mozzarella balls, too. But he realized his goals were too ambitious for a one-person operation. So, he pared the focus to cheddar curds, brie, and blue. "I had to choose the best sellers and what I want to be known for. We've been known for our cheddars since Grandpa's time," he says.

It's a seven-day-a-week business, with up to 12-hour workdays. Even during the pandemic in 2020, Schroeder continued his work routine, though sales outlets were few. He gave away some of the cheese to local food pantries.

Bryon's wife, Angela, also plays a role in the business. In addition to working full-time at Lands' End in Dodgeville, Angela handles the Schroeder Käse paperwork, including the company's permits and licenses.

"I've always dreamt about doing all of this," Bryon says. "When I was growing up, I looked up to my grandfather, my dad, and my uncles. I wanted to do what they did when I got older, and here I am doing it. I never second-guessed it."

MAKING WISCONSIN BRIE

Schroeder Käse gets all of its milk from a single farm that grazes Holstein and Jersey cows in the summer and feeds the animals hay in the winter. "It's higher-fat milk. That's what we wanted," Schroeder says.

The triple-crème brie is a soft, smooth cow's milk cheese with extra cream added just before pasteurization, and in one popular version of it, a line of vegetable ash runs through the middle.

To make the brie, the cheese is hand-poured into forms, brined in tanks, and wheeled into curing rooms with very specific moisture and temperature levels. The racks are flipped every day—even on Sundays—and aged seven to ten days before being hand-wrapped. "To get that nice white mold on the outside, you have to watch it carefully, to wait for the moisture to dry down and the mold to develop on those wheels. You have to monitor the cheese every day," Schroeder says.

"We don't take vacations," he adds.

The vegetable ash comes from a supplier and consists of a blend of dried vegetables that are crushed into a powder. Schroeder had seen photos of the ash product and thought he might experiment with it. After some trial batches, "it worked out pretty well, so we ran with it," he says.

"Worked out pretty well" might be an understatement—or a sign of Schroeder's modesty. Schroeder Käse's triple-crème brie was one of the Driftless cheeses featured on *Top Chef: Wisconsin*. The contestant who used the brie didn't win that round of the competition, but it wasn't the fault of the cheese. Rather, the chef was called out for masking its flavor with too much breading.

Seeing Schroeder Käse's cheese get the star treatment on a nationally broadcast TV program was pretty exciting, Bryon and Angela agree.

"It was really neat! And it was good to have some national exposure on such a highly watched show, for our small footprint to be recognized on something like that," Angela says.

The family watched the episode from their home when it aired. "It was nice to put our cheese up there with the more well-known cheese companies," says Bryon.

Customers at the Dane County Farmers' Market in Madison watched the program, too. "We got a lot of feedback from people at the market. A lot of local people came up to us and told us how happy they were to see our product on the show. Feedback from actual customers means a lot to us," Bryon says.

Sales of the brie traditionally jump during the holiday season, Angela adds. "A lot of people score it, bake it, and put honey and pecans or walnuts on top, or they bake it in a puff pastry. Some make brie bites with preserves and puff pastry. And it's great on the charcuterie board."

BLUE CHEESE, TOO

Schroeder Käse also makes a double-crème gorgonzola blue cheese, a process that takes four or five days. Once the cheese is formed, it is dry-salted and dipped into a mold prevention solution to keep mold from growing on the outside of the wheels. The rounds are then pierced with stainless-steel needles to allow different molds to grow inside the wheels, creating the blue veins and sharp flavor. The blue cheese ages for six to nine months before it goes to market.

A good blue cheese gains flavor as it ages, but on top of that, adding double and triple crème "elevated it," Bryon says. "A regular blue cheese, with standard milk, is more crumbly and lower fat. Ours is more spreadable."

The brie and the blue do not share the same space. They are aged in separate curing rooms. "Because the temperatures and the types of mold are different. We don't want the two molds together," Bryon says.

While cheese is the mainstay of Bryon's heritage, it is no longer his company's sole product. In 2023, he launched a line of drinkable yogurt. The equipment, purchased from a former purveyor, is housed in a semi-trailer that sits outside the Schroeder Käse cheese factory in Darlington. Schroeder calls it a "cheese on wheels unit."

The main destination for the drinkable yogurt is the Dane County Farmers' Market, which is held around the Wisconsin State Capitol building in Madison on Saturday mornings from mid-April through early November and then moves to indoor facilities.

Schroeder already was selling his cheese there, so it was a natural addition. "There was nothing to drink up there. I thought, *Why not do something different and come up with something healthy?* You can walk around [the Capitol Square] and drink it," Schroeder says.

For the 2024 market, Schroeder Käse offered 12 flavors of drinkable yogurt, including tropical fruit such as mango and pineapple, as well as more standard yogurt varieties, like strawberry and blueberry. The flavors are made with syrups; using fresh fruit would sharply shorten the shelf life of the beverages, Schroeder says.

Drinkable yogurt is a highly regulated process, even more than for cheese. The facility needs to meet more stringent requirements set by the government. Schroeder Käse's trailer and equipment are inspected by the state every three months, samples of yogurt and raw milk are tested monthly, and state fees are much higher than for cheese due to those additional regulations.

"But we have a lot of happy customers, so it's worth it," Schroeder says.

A FAMILY EFFORT

Schroeder Käse doesn't have a shop and doesn't take online orders. Shipping cheese would require keeping it cold, and curds would no longer be as fresh by the time the shipment arrived, Bryon says.

Distributors get the cheeses to stores around Wisconsin, and the Schroeder Käse booth is always at the Dane County Farmers' Market.

Staffing the booth is a family affair. Bryon and Angela, their daughter, Kassidy, and son, Cameron, greet customers and sell the company's dairy products. Drinkable yogurt and cheese curds are big sellers.

Angela, who grew up in Montfort, confides that the curds are her favorite of the company's products. "I like the white curds. In our area, everyone wants the yellow curds, but I like the white better, with no added color. I do think the white are a little sweeter. When you get them when they're warm, right out of the vat, there's something about the saltiness and the squeak of the fresh curds," she says.

Angela says she can see Cameron's pride in becoming a part of the family cheesemaking tradition. "He gets excited when customers tell him how much they like the products," she says.

Back at the factory, Cameron cuts the cheese for packaging, flips the cheese racks, and helps sanitize the equipment. "It's pretty fun," he says. "I like the way everything comes together [in the cheesemaking process], and the cheese is the final result."

Some days, Cameron works from 3 a.m. to 7:30 p.m. "It's all right; I don't have an issue with working. My father's favorite words are: 'It won't get done by itself,'" he says. Cameron hopes to earn his own cheesemaker's license in 2025.

How does a small, two-person cheesemaking operation survive in a business world where the trend seems to be "bigger is better"? "Just having the knowledge [of cheesemaking] and the connections I've made through the years," Bryon says. "I think we're doing pretty well."

Bryon and Cameron have visions of growing the business, building a larger cheese plant closer to their home, and opening a retail shop where customers could buy their cheeses and yogurt drinks—hopefully, within the next five years.

"When my family sold the [legacy] cheese plant, we lost something. Now, we've gained it back. I'm happy my son is on board and will carry on the family business," Bryon says.

Angela shares that sentiment. "There's something different about being in Wisconsin, where you have to be licensed as a cheesemaker. There are such strict regulations; no other state has that.

"They have a right to bust their chest out a little and be proud of what they've accomplished," she says.

. . . .

Name: Schroeder Käse

Owner: Cheesemaker Bryon Schroeder

Community: Darlington

Established: 2016

Facebook page: www.facebook.com/p/Schroeder-Kase-100063470435370

Retail shop: None

Email: scheese4@yahoo.com

Tours: None

. . . .

Wisconsin Master Cheesemakers in our book: Sid Cook, Andy Hatch, Tony Hook, Chris Roelli, Bob Wills: https://www.wisconsincheese.com/our-cheese/our-makers/wisconsin-master-cheesemakers

UPLANDS CHEESE
ANDY HATCH

189

Wisconsin Master Cheesemaker Andy Hatch steps over a fence and onto green pasture at the top of a hill at Uplands Cheese, north of Dodgeville. Cows of different colors—dark brown, caramel, and white with black splotches—shyly approach him, seeking a rub on the head or maybe a treat to eat.

"We tend to have nicknames for our favorite 20 or 30 cows in the herd. My perennial favorites are Coco and Flora and Sideways Sally. Whenever I'm out in the field, we end up finding each other," Hatch says.

They are part of a special herd of 190 cows. Their pedigree is unique, and their milk—and theirs alone—is used to make one of the most prestigious cheeses produced in Wisconsin: Uplands Cheese's Pleasant Ridge Reserve. A hard, aged, Alpine-style cheese with a golden color and a rich, savory, complex taste, Pleasant Ridge is named after the land formation on which the farm sits.

It has received more awards than any other cheese in U.S. history. It is the only cheese to be named Best of Show in the American Cheese Society competition three times, in 2001, 2005, and 2010, and the only cheese that's also won Best of Show at the U.S. Cheese Championship in 2003. Most recently, Pleasant Ridge won first place in two categories in the 2024 American Cheese Society contest.

Uplands Cheese only makes one other cheese, Rush Creek Reserve, a soft-ripened, washed-rind cheese that ages for two months, its rounds bound with spruce bark. It's also made with milk that only comes from Uplands' cows.

"The goal is quality. We control every aspect of the product. We try to make cheese that tastes like our farm," Hatch says.

Food & Wine magazine lists Uplands Cheese as one of the Top 50 U.S. Cheesemakers. A 2021 article says Pleasant Ridge Reserve is "one of the best European-style mountain cheeses on these shores" while Rush Creek Reserve is called "a high-profile stunner … that showed us just what we Americans were actually capable of."[1]

Feld restaurant in Chicago showcased the two Uplands cheeses in a special dinner that featured them in all but three of the more than 20 courses. The meal started with chicken broth infused with Pleasant Ridge rinds and proceeded with other courses that included cheese crisps; pâte à choux with cheese mousse; French onion soup with Rush Creek on a rye crostini, blowtorched until gooey; lobster ravioli in a sauce with both cheeses; and shortbread cookies with Pleasant Ridge.

---

1   David Landsel, "The Best Cheese in America: These Are the Top 50 U.S. Cheese-makers," *Food & Wine*, December 27, 2021, https://www.foodandwine.com/lifestyle/best-cheese-america.

On the regular nightly menu, Feld owner and Chef Jake Potashnick offers warmed Rush Creek poured tableside over roasted parsnip ice cream—at least, until the batch of cheese runs out.

Potashnick had visited Uplands during the production of Rush Creek, and Hatch showed him around the fields and the factory. "It caught me off guard how unbelievable it was, and how thoughtful a guy Andy is," Potashnick says. "He has a very old-school, European mindset about approaching his product that requires a certain level of purity of heart. I think that's a lot of what makes him special."

Hatch says his mission is threefold: "I want to make something delicious and bring people joy. I want to make something that reflects the nature of our farm. And I'm trying to do something meaningful in terms of sustainable agriculture and rural economic development, to show people that farming responsibly can produce something that is economically viable and is also delicious."

But as seriously as he takes his cheesemaking—and he takes it very seriously—Hatch is a humble, low-key guy who plays mandolin in a local band in his free time and boasts proudly about his wife. Caitlin Leline Hatch is a watercolor artist whose paintings of horses and farm animals are sold in galleries in Door County and in Santa Fe, New Mexico.

"I'm not the most talented person in the family," Andy says.

THE OLD-WORLD WAY

Uplands Cheese is a throwback to old-world cheesemaking. It is a farmstead cheese plant on land where cows have been milked for more than a century.

Not only does Hatch make only two cheeses, using milk that's solely from Uplands' cows, but he has strict standards on when those cheeses are made.

Pleasant Ridge Reserve is made only when the cows eat fresh pasture grasses, April/May through November/December.

Rush Creek Reserve is made only in the fall, when the cows' diet also incorporates hay.

The cows live outdoors year-round, and they are moved to a different five- to ten-acre section of the hilly slopes several times a day—a practice called rotational grazing—so that the vegetation they eat is always fresh.

Uplands uses unpasteurized milk for its two cheeses. Unpasteurized milk makes for richer, more complex flavors in cheese because there's a broader range of microbes available to ferment the cheese, Hatch says.

While concerns have been raised about drinking raw milk, using it in cheese is absolutely safe, he says. "There are hundreds of years of proof of that. Cheesemaking is designed to preserve milk and make it safe. It is different from fluid raw milk that offers no protection from possible pathogens."

UPLANDS HISTORY

Andy and Caitlin co-own Uplands Cheese with Scott Mericka and his wife, Liana, who is a nurse. Andy makes the cheese, and Scott handles the herd. The two families bought the 500-acre, Iowa County property in 2014 after serving as apprentices under the former owners, Uplands Cheese founders Mike and Carol Gingrich and Dan and Jeanne Patenaude, who set the business on its path.

The Gingriches and the Patenaudes purchased the farm in 1994 and began using rotational grazing. Realizing that the unglaciated, rolling hills of the Driftless region produced diverse grasses, flowers, and herbs that made their cows' milk special, they worked with the UW–Madison's Center for Dairy Research to develop a cheese based on those made in the French and Swiss Alps. The result was Pleasant Ridge Reserve.

Andy and Scott have added their own marks of distinction by evolving the genetics of their unique herd of cows, improving pasture management, and refining cheesemaking techniques. Their cows are not the typical Wisconsin black-and-white Holstein dairy cows, but rather, they are a mixed breed of Uplands' making, including Friesian, Ayrshire, Jersey, and Montbéliarde. "They are much smaller than Holsteins, and they are more athletic. Our cows live outside year-round, so they have a lot of hardiness and athleticism; they climb up and down hills in the heat and in the snow," Andy says.

"Our form of dairying is very unique to our region, especially with farmstead cheese," Scott says. "We use a lot of farm management systems that you would find in New Zealand."

Mericka milks the cows from early spring through mid-January. "They dry off in the winter when the grass isn't growing and have, at minimum, a 60-day break from milking," he says.

He is very methodical about where the cows graze on the farm's layered ridges, and for how long. "Every week, we measure our pastures. The biomass measurement of all the available feed becomes our grazing wedge. We use a sonar reader that tells us how much grass is available," Mericka says. "We're trying to manage the rate at which the grass is growing and the rate at which the cows are eating the grass to give the cows the right phase of growth every single day."

Uplands is part of a multi-year grant project with the Dairy Grazing Alliance, which is developing technology to measure and map biomass production for grazing dairies, Mericka says.

"We are also trying to correlate the production of above-ground biomass with the soil's capacity to sequester carbon as a climate change mitigation strategy."

Because the cows move from one part of the farm to another, what they eat may vary from one day to the next. That affects the flavor of their milk, and as a result, the cheese can taste different each day. "It's really like making a different vintage of wine every day. Both are expressions of terroir," Hatch says. "It makes cheesemaking very interesting to have a product that reflects that kind of nuance and sensitivity to the farm itself. Customers are receiving something singular: cheese from one day's milk, from one herd of cows on one farm. It's a special thing."

Hatch welcomes cheesemongers to come to the Uplands creamery and sample different wheels of Pleasant Ridge, produced on different dates, and then choose their favorites.

Ken Monteleone, owner of Fromagination in Madison, says that when he opened his cheese shop in 2007, instead of a ribbon cutting, he cut into a wheel of Pleasant Ridge Reserve. "It is our top-selling cheese, 17 years in a row. Andy hand-selects our wheel for us and ships it directly to our shop," he says.

L'Etoile owner and Chef Tory Miller says the haute cuisine Madison restaurant was Uplands' first restaurant customer. "We absolutely love both of the cheeses they make. We love to taste each vintage and see how the cheeses evolve and change with the seasons," he says. "The Uplands milk has a very distinct tropical note that, to me, makes their cheeses stand apart as unmistakably their own."

INSIDE UPLANDS

The Uplands Cheese plant is housed in a simple, white building with green trim. The only identifying marker is a small, gray sign next to the front door. The engraved wood panel shows a drawing of a cow accompanied by a woman carrying a bucket of milk; it is captioned Uplands Cheese. The image was taken from a wood carving made by artist Audrey Christie, who lived down the road. The sign was made by computer about 25 years ago. "We thought it would be cool to take it back to wood. Now, it's our logo," Hatch says.

In the production room, cheesemakers employ the same techniques as their counterparts did 100 years ago. For both cheeses, "we use a small, open vat, and we make one vat a day with that day's fresh milk, entirely by hand. Pleasant Ridge Reserve ages in open air on wooden boards for about one year. We constantly wipe down the natural rind with saltwater to protect the cheese and develop the flavor," Hatch says.

Pleasant Ridge Reserve is known for its unique flavor. "It has a savory richness that, to me, is reminiscent of chicken or beef broth, an umami richness that you don't find in pasteurized cheese made through industrial production. It may have a floral or tropical fruit finish," Hatch says. "And when you taste a different batch, you're tasting a different 10 acres of pasture."

During a visit to the plant in September, Rush Creek Reserve was in production. "This was fresh milk at 7:30 this morning," Hatch said, and later explained the process. "It acidifies slowly overnight, is brined the following morning, and we wrap each one in strips of boiled bark. Then it is brushed with brine, by hand, every day. After two weeks, we stop brushing it and let the mold grow." Rush Creek ages for about two months and is sold in November and December.

Hatch learned how to make the soft cheese in France and then created his own recipe. It's based on a famous French cheese, Vacherin Mont d'Or, that's been produced in the foothills of the Alps—only during the winter months—since the 13th century.

In France, the cheese is eaten after it ages for 25 to 30 days. In the U.S., though, cheese made from unpasteurized milk must be aged for at least 60 days.

"I had to transform the recipe, almost from top to bottom," Hatch says. "For the entire first year, we threw every batch away. Then in 2010, we released it for the first time. *The New York Times* covered it. It was like getting shot out of a cannon. Everybody wanted the cheese, and it's really never changed."

To eat Rush Creek, the top rind is traditionally cut off, and the soft and custardy, savory and smoky cheese inside is scooped out with a spoon. "The taste is very rich, almost meaty like ham or bacon," Hatch says.

Milwaukee Chef Dan Jacobs says Rush Creek is a tradition for him. "Every year we do something with Rush Creek. It is an annual affair at the restaurant, and it's always fun." Jacobs is co-owner of EsterEv and DanDan restaurants and was runner-up in Bravo TV's *Top Chef: Wisconsin* series in 2024.

L'Etoile's Miller says Rush Creek "continues to be a shining star

in the lineup of special cheeses from Wisconsin. We call it 'Rush Creekmas' the first day it arrives in our kitchen in the fall."

Bon Appétit lists both of Uplands' cheeses among the 25 most important cheeses in America, according to a 2018 article that quoted cheese experts. Of Rush Creek Reserve, Ari Weinzweig wrote: "Rush Creek is hard to make but easy to eat … a darned delicious cheese!" And Tia Keenan said, "If cheese could be pudding, it'd be Rush Creek Reserve. I'm a texture queen and this is my jam."[2]

Will Uplands ever make a third cheese? "It's very possible. We have no philosophical objection to that, but we can't meet demand for the existing two," Hatch says. "Maybe someday if we expand our facilities and need to sell some more cheese to pay for that, yes, we would consider it."

FARMING DREAMS

Andy doesn't have a cheesemaking background, or even a farming background. He grew up outside Milwaukee. His father was a lawyer and his mother, a milliner. "But my family was pretty serious about food," he says.

He felt drawn to agriculture in his youth. "I had the farming bug as a teenager. It was a pastoral fantasy," he says. He earned a degree in anthropology from Trinity College in Connecticut and a certificate in dairy science at UW–Madison. His dream took him to Europe, where he learned the craft of cheesemaking as an apprentice in France, Italy, Germany, Norway, and Ireland.

Scott studied agronomy and grass-based dairy farming at Warren Wilson College in Asheville, North Carolina, an agricultural college with a working farm.

---

2   Carey Polis, "25 Most Important Cheeses of America, According to Cheese Experts," *Bon Appétit*, April 25, 2018, https://www.bonappetit.com/gallery/most-important-chees-es-in-america?srsltid=AfmBOoodln_5IUa5ig_joqXf7YVzAuJwdTpDlzZoDLQMX9_NBIHFaM5R.

Andy says Uplands' location in the Driftless region is critical to its success. "These hills in the Driftless are very difficult for growing crops, but grass grows wonderfully here. There's something about the soil, the topography, the rainfall patterns, and the character of the water. We have wells that are 750 feet deep, way down into the limestone, and the water is spectacular. Water has a lot of influence on the food that's made with it.

"The conditions here have created something special. I see our cheese as a harvest of this place more than I see it as a manufactured product," he says.

TOP CHEF CELEBRITY

Andy Hatch was one of the few Wisconsin cheesemakers who played a role—beyond his cheese—on the *Top Chef: Wisconsin* cheese episode. He and Pam Hodgson of Sartori Cheese in Plymouth introduced the selection of cheeses that the chef-contestants would have to work with.

Uplands cheese also starred in the episode's main challenge as Chef Michelle Wallace's Pleasant Ridge potato fritter over collard greens won the event.

The nationally broadcast program acted like fireworks for Wisconsin cheesemakers. Three weeks after the episode aired, Hatch told the *Wisconsin State Journal* that his website sales were up 3,792 percent, which means 700 new customers had ordered 1,100 pounds of cheese.

Hatch admits he had some initial qualms about participating in *Top Chef*, but they were put to rest. "I really enjoyed the filming. I don't watch the show, or really any TV, and at first, I made the lazy assumption that it'd be an ego-soaked charade—reality TV posing as reality. But the judges were genuine and cared about the food and the chefs, and of course, the chefs themselves were the real deal. They are hardworking people passionate about their craft," he says.

He was also encouraged by the show's concept. "It was pretty inspiring to see television celebrating people who do real work with their hands … I really admire that they took the time to find small, interesting cheese producers."

STAYING HUMBLE

Uplands Cheese does not have a retail store and it sits up a gravel driveway, off the highway. So, when unexpected customers make their way to the cheese plant, it's a bit of a surprise. On a day last fall, a carload of visitors from the West Coast had found their way to the site, seeking to buy some cheese. Andy let them in and politely sold them a wedge. "I'm so Midwestern about it," he says.

For Hatch, the success of Uplands Cheese does not just benefit the two owners' families; its impact reverberates through the Dodgeville area and throughout the Driftless.

"Uplands spends more than $1 million a year in this neighborhood, and that is a really important part of what we're doing. It goes to suppliers, wages to our employees, feed for our cows, veterinarians, electricians, and plumbers," Hatch says.

Then, customers from around the U.S. buy gift boxes of Uplands cheeses and products made by other Driftless businesses— sausages, crackers, and preserves.

"We are harvesting that cash and bringing it back to Iowa County and spending it here where there isn't as much disposable income," Hatch says.

"There is such a deep tradition here of cheesemaking and importing money. We are exporting pride."

Name: Uplands Cheese

Owners: Caitlin and Wisconsin Master Cheesemaker Andy Hatch; Liana and dairyman Scott Mericka

Community: Pleasant Ridge, near Dodgeville

Established: 2000

Website: uplandscheese.com

Retail shop: None, but people wishing to visit to buy cheese are encouraged to call or email the creamery.

Email: orders@uplandscheese.com

Phone: 608-935-5558

Tours and/or public events: None

Five of the 12 cheesemakers in our book had their cheeses featured on Bravo TV's *Top Chef: Wisconsi*n in 2024: Roelli Cheese Haus, Uplands Cheese, Schroeder Käse, Hook's Cheese, and Carr Valley Cheese.

HOW TO CHEESE

 ## SELECTING

The best places to buy cheese are a specialty cheese shop or directly from the producer at their factory store or a farmers' market. But if those aren't options, don't worry; grocery store cheese counters have improved significantly over the last few years, and a good grocery store will have knowledgeable staff and a varied selection of cheeses.

When selecting cheese, first consider what you'll be using it for. For a cheese board, aim for a variety of textures, milk types, and flavors, such as a creamy brie, a sharp aged cheddar, a tangy blue cheese, and a nutty alpine-style cheese, or select a set of similar cheeses, such as cheddars of different ages. If you are cooking with the cheese, select one that matches the characteristics of the cheese used in the recipe. Pleasant Ridge is great melted on top of French onion soup, two-year cheddar makes a wonderful grilled cheese, Nordic Creamery mozzarella is perfect on pizza, and Pecora Nocciola is the ideal topping for a plate of pasta.

Timing is essential for quality. Purchase cheese as close as possible to when you plan to serve or use it. Soft cheeses are best enjoyed fresh and should be consumed within a few days of purchase. Harder cheeses have a longer shelf life but should still be stored properly and used promptly to preserve their quality.

Quantity is another key factor. For a cheese board, plan on one to two ounces of cheese per person per variety to ensure everyone gets a taste without excessive leftovers. Remember that cheese is perishable, so buy only what you can use within its optimal timeframe.

Finally, building a relationship with a cheesemonger can have big advantages. Their recommendations, tailored to your taste preferences, dietary needs, and the occasion, can save time and ensure a satisfying experience. They may also share insider tips on new arrivals, seasonal specialties, and pairings.

 SERVING

One of the most important considerations when serving cheese is how to cut it. Each type of cheese has its optimal method to ensure even portions and preserve its structure. For soft cheeses like triple-crème brie or Pavé Henri, use a soft cheese knife or a wire cutter to maintain their creamy texture while creating clean slices. Hard cheeses like Red Rock or bandaged cheddar benefit from a sturdy knife or a cheese plane, which allows you to shave off thin, manageable pieces. For blue cheeses like Little Boy Blue, a cheese knife with holes or a narrow blade helps to minimize sticking and preserve the cheese's delicate veins. Always cut from the center outward, ensuring each piece has a bit of the rind and the interior for a balanced flavor experience.

Some cheeses will have special serving requirements. Rush Creek is wrapped in a strip of spruce bark so it can't be cut into wedges; the conventional way to serve it is to cut the "lid" off of the wheel and peel it back. A grilling cheese like Brun-Uusto or Coalho will usually be grilled or pan fried and then skewered or cubed for serving.

Temperature plays a crucial role in bringing out the best in cheese. It should be served at room temperature to allow its flavors and aromas to fully develop. Remove cheese from the refrigerator about 30 minutes before serving, depending on its firmness. Softer cheeses warm up more quickly, while harder cheeses take longer. Serving cheese too cold can mute its flavor, but letting it sit out for too long or get too warm can cause it to lose its texture and freshness.

Visual appeal is another key factor when serving cheese. A well-thought-out presentation not only makes the cheese look inviting but also helps guide your guests through the tasting experience. Arrange cheeses on a wooden board, slate, or marble slab. Group cheeses by type or texture, and use labels or markers to identify each, especially if you're serving lesser-known varieties. Garnish the board with seasonal fruits like grapes, figs, or apple slices, and add a touch of greenery with fresh herbs. Nuts, dried fruits, and edible flowers can also enhance your presentation's visual and textural appeal.

Pairing cheese with the right accompaniments elevates the overall experience. Bread and crackers are classic choices, providing a neutral base that lets the cheese shine. Opt for a variety of textures, such as crusty baguette slices, crisp flatbreads, or lightly salted crackers. Sweet accompaniments like honey, fruit preserves, and chutneys complement the richness of cheese, while savory options like olives, cured meats, and pickles add depth and contrast. Beverages are equally important. Wine is a traditional favorite, but craft beer, cider, or even tea can pair beautifully with different cheeses. Consider the flavors and intensity of the cheese and the beverage to find harmonious pairings.

Finally, consider the ambiance of your presentation. Serving cheese is as much about the atmosphere as it is about the food. Use lighting, table settings, and music to create a welcoming environment. Whether you're hosting an intimate gathering or a larger celebration, how you present and serve cheese can set the tone for the event. By paying attention to the details—from cutting and arranging to pairing and plating—you can ensure that your cheese offering becomes a memorable centerpiece of any occasion.

TASTING

The tasting process begins with your eyes. Take a moment to observe the cheese's appearance, noting its color, texture, and any distinctive features. A bloomy rind on a brie, the veining in a blue cheese, or the crystalline flecks in an aged gouda all tell a story about the cheese's character and production. Visual inspection sets expectations for your other senses, giving you a baseline to make comparisons. For example, you may think, *It looks so creamy. I didn't expect the flavor to be so sharp.*

Next, use your sense of smell. Bring the cheese close to your nose and inhale deeply, identifying the aromas. A cheese may carry creamy, earthy, nutty, fruity, floral, grassy, caramel, sharp, sour, or even barnyard-y notes, depending on its type and aging process.

As you take your first bite, let the cheese linger on your tongue to fully experience its texture and taste. Notice whether it is creamy or crumbly, dense or airy. Allow the cheese to warm slightly in your mouth, as this can release additional flavors. Pay attention to the balance of saltiness, sweetness, acidity, and umami, as well as any evolving layers of complexity.

Don't forget to savor the moment. Tasting cheese is not a rushed activity but a deliberate exploration of craftsmanship and tradition. Whether you're enjoying a solo tasting or sharing the experience with friends, let each bite remind you of the skill and care that goes into creating cheese. By engaging all your senses and approaching the process with curiosity, you can uncover new favorites and develop a lasting appreciation for this versatile and beloved food.

STORING

Cheese was invented as a way to store and preserve milk, so you would be forgiven for thinking you don't need to take care when storing cheese. Proper cheese storage preserves its flavor and texture. While fresh cheeses like ricotta, feta, and mozzarella are best kept in their original containers, most other cheeses benefit from breathable wrapping. Cheese paper is the best choice for wrapping cheese, but parchment or wax paper works well too. Avoid using plastic wrap or plastic bags, as they trap moisture at the surface of the cheese which can cause it to go bad faster, and plastic can also impact an unappealing flavor to the cheese over time.

Keep other fresh cheeses like ricotta, mascarpone, and burrata in their original containers with the lid tightly sealed and consume them quickly, typically within a week of opening. Discard if moldy or sour-smelling.

Storage temperature and humidity greatly affect how long you can keep cheese. Cheese should be stored in the refrigerator, ideally in the vegetable crisper or a dedicated cheese drawer, where the temperature is consistent and slightly more humid. Aim for 35°F to 45°F (1°C to 7°C). Avoid freezing cheese or storing it against the fridge's coldest spots, as this can alter its texture and flavor.

TROUBLESHOOTING

 ## MY CHEESE SMELLS LIKE AMMONIA

A strong ammonia scent coming from your cheese can be unpleasant, but it doesn't necessarily mean the cheese has to be discarded. This odor is a natural byproduct of surface-ripened cheeses like brie and Camembert as they age. Unwrap the cheese and let it breathe for 15 minutes. If the smell dissipates, it's fine to eat the cheese. If the smell continues to linger, or the cheese has an acrid flavor, it's time to discard it. Always trust your taste buds—a slight ammonia smell may not ruin the flavor, so a small taste test can help you decide.

 ## MY CHEESE IS MOLDY

When mold appears on cheese, it's important to assess the type of cheese and the mold's location. Soft cheeses, like cream cheese or brie, should be discarded if mold develops, as it can spread internally. In contrast, hard cheeses like cheddar or Parmesan can often be salvaged by cutting away the moldy area, removing all of it, and not running the knife through the mold. If you are consistently getting mold on your cheese, reread the section on proper cheese storage or make an effort to consume cheese faster.

 ## MY CHEESE SWEATS

If your cheese is sweating after being served, it may simply have gotten too warm. Blot it with a paper towel and return it to the refrigerator briefly to cool it down. If it is sweating in the refrigerator, this is a sign that the cheese isn't stored properly (consult the section on storage to avoid).

MY CHEESE ISN'T MELTING PROPERLY

Not all cheeses are made equally when it comes to melting. Some cheeses, like paneer and Halloumi, don't melt at all; they brown and crisp similarly to meat. Other cheeses with low moisture and low fat content, like Parmesan, can be melted but harden again upon cooling (great for making gluten-free cheese crackers). Many other cheeses, like mozzarella, melt and stay soft and gooey.

If you want to make a cheese sauce, the key is stabilization. Cheese sauce is an emulsion of fat and water, stabilized by proteins (and often starches), and to make a great sauce, you need to get the ratio of those elements correct and mix them together carefully. But there are a couple of tricks to make life easier. The easiest is to use an emulsifying salt like sodium citrate, which will bind the fat and water together and make the process so easy it almost feels like cheating. Another option is to add evaporated skim milk to your sauce, which will add proteins but not much water or fat, improving the strength of the emulsion. If you are still having trouble with your sauce, add a little acid, like lemon juice. The lower pH will help the formation of the emulsion. And, whatever you do, don't use pre-shredded cheese to make a sauce. Those cheeses often have anti-clumping chemicals on them that can interfere with the emulsion.

 MY CHEESE DRIED OUT

Grate your dry cheese and use it for topping dishes like pasta or soup, or incorporate it with other cheese in recipes where it will be melted.

MY CHEESE HAS CRYSTALS IN IT

Crunchy crystals in aged cheeses like gouda or Parmesan are often misunderstood. If they are crunchy, white crystals in the cheese's interior are made from tyrosine, an amino acid. If they are softer, off-white, and found primarily on the outside of the cheese, they are made from calcium lactate. A cheese might have both kinds of crystals. Either way, they are harmless and a sign of well-aged, high-quality cheese. Instead of viewing them as a flaw, consider them a textural bonus.

MY CHEESE TASTES BLAND

Bland cheese doesn't have to remain lackluster. Pairing it with bold accompaniments such as honey, mustard, or fresh herbs can enhance its flavor. A pinch of salt or black pepper can also bring out the cheese's natural taste. Gentle warming through melting or grilling can reveal hidden complexity for some cheeses. If it's a younger cheese, allowing it to age further in your fridge may help it develop more character.

MY CHEESE IS SLIMY

If the sliminess is due to condensation or improper wrapping, wipe the cheese with a clean, dry cloth. If the texture is accompanied by an off smell or taste, it's better to discard the cheese.

In 1922, the number of cheese plants operating in Wisconsin peaked at 2,807.

CONTRIBUTORS

 **JUDY NEWMAN COBURN** is a freelance writer and editor in Madison. She is a former business reporter for the *Wisconsin State Journal* and a former radio reporter/anchor, and has a degree in journalism from Northwestern University's Medill School of Journalism.

Thanks to this project, Judy has gained a deep appreciation of artisanal Driftless cheese and a boundless appetite for it.

 PAUL STRABBING is a Chicago-based commercial food photographer with an enthusiastic love for Wisconsin cheesemakers (and their cows, goats, and sheep)! Meeting these cheesemakers and photographing their stories has been a highlight of his 25-year career, which includes a James Beard Award-winning cookbook project with Jacquy Pfeiffer, *The Art of French Pastry*. Paul is also the official photographer for the Club Coupe du Monde Team USA pastry team, competing in Lyon, France in 2027.

 **NICOLE BUJEWSKI** has a profound love for the sweeter side of the kitchen. She is a pastry chef who trained and then taught at the prestigious French Pastry School in Chicago and owned and operated leFlour, a neighborhood bakery in Chicago.

Nicole founded The Book Kitchen, inside the Republic of Letters bookstore in Mineral Point, in 2024. At The Book Kitchen, Nicole shares her knowledge and love for the culinary arts with students and enthusiasts, creating a bridge among her passions—food, teaching, and literature.

KEITH BURROWS is a scientist and writer who has lived in the Driftless Area since 2007. His writing has appeared in *Driftless Appetite* (which he co-founded), the *Voice of the River Valley*, *Contours*, *Imagine 2074*, and *Arts Midwest*.

In 2023, Keith opened the Republic of Letters bookstore in Mineral Point with Leslie Damaso. The mission of Republic of Letters is to be a home for creativity and celebration, to foster community engagement and shared learning, and to connect readers to books that will change their lives.

LESLIE DAMASO is a Filipino-American singer, musician, visual artist, poet, writer, teacher and owner at Buttonhill Music Studio and Republic of Letters books. For eighteen years, Leslie has explored and celebrated the beauty of the Driftless through her writing and various artistic expressions. Her curiosity and deep friendships, especially with the people who make this place, makes her proud to call this her home.

KRISTIN MITCHELL an accomplished graphic designer with more than 30 years of experience, expanded her Mineral Point-based design business in 2011 by founding Little Creek Press, an independent publishing division dedicated to producing high-quality books of outstanding literary merit.

In 2024, Little Creek Press refocused on showcasing Wisconsin-centered books and authors, celebrating the Midwest's rich storytelling tradition. This key project, *The Wisconsin Whey*, highlights the state's iconic cheese industry and the dedicated artisans behind it.

SPECIAL CONTRIBUTORS: Krista Loomans and Susan Parenti

Uplands Cheese
Landmark Creamery